Deaf Persons
in
Professional Employment

Deaf Persons
in
Professional Employment

By

ALAN B. CRAMMATTE, M.A.
Associate Professor of Business Administration
Gallaudet College
Washington, D.C.

CHARLES C THOMAS · PUBLISHER
Springfield · Illinois · U.S.A.

Published and Distributed Throughout the World by
CHARLES C THOMAS · PUBLISHER
BANNERSTONE HOUSE
301-327 East Lawrence Avenue, Springfield, Illinois, U.S.A.
NATCHEZ PLANTATION HOUSE
735 North Atlantic Boulevard, Fort Lauderdale, Florida, U.S.A.

With THOMAS BOOKS *careful attention is given to all details of
manufacturing and design. It is the Publisher's desire to present books
that are satisfactory as to their physical qualities and artistic possibilities
and appropriate for their particular use.* THOMAS BOOKS *will be true
to those laws of quality that assure a good name and good will.*

Printed in the United States of America
H-2

To Boyce R. Williams

INTRODUCTION

This REPORT DEALS WITH deaf persons employed in professional occupations, a rare and anomalous group of workers. They are rare, for the nearest thing to a census of the deaf population[2]* revealed only 6.6 per cent of all the 7,920 employed deaf respondents to be in professional, technical and kindred occupations as compared to 10.6 per cent of the general United States population so employed. In addition, more than half of this 6.6 per cent was engaged in teaching and ministering to other deaf people, laudable occupations but not particularly challenging in a professional sense. The deaf professional workers are anomalous because they are handicapped in communication but yet are making their careers in occupations which require more than a little communication, dealing as they do with ideas and people rather than with tools and raw materials only.

The literature on education and rehabilitation of deaf persons has for years been concerned mainly with the disabilities and the problems of deafness. Education, vocational training and job placement have emphasized the lower levels of employment rather than optimum accomplishments. Almost since establishment, schools for the deaf have trained their pupils in the manual trades. As the blind were taught to weave and to make brooms, so the deaf were trained in printing, carpentry, cooking and sewing. Yet some deaf persons, despite the double handicap of deafness and of stereotyped views of their abilities by the general public, have managed to make their way into occupations demanding higher skills and offering greater rewards than do the manual trades. Although they have thus demonstrated the fitness of some deaf persons for higher occupations, the impact of the demonstration is dulled by the fact that it has been recognized only in subjective, inspirational writing of limited circulation. Definitive knowledge of these occupational potentials has been virtually nonexistent, despite increasing interest in the full utilization of deaf manpower.

*Superior numbers refer to the selected bibliography on page 163.

One implication of such a situation was clear: More opportunities for deaf persons might exist if systematic knowledge were available concerning the experiences of those employed in professional occupations—how they had met and solved the problems arising from their handicap. Such knowledge would be of value in the guidance of deaf persons with aspirations and qualifications for these occupations. For rehabilitation workers and trainees, it would round out their general knowledge with specific information covering maximum potentials and the highest attainable goals as well as disabilities and frustrations. Thus, it was hoped that the study would be a first step in the accumulation and analysis of information about opportunities for the hearing-impaired in professional employment.

WHAT IS A PROFESSION?

Before attempting to study a deaf professional person, it is necessary to consider the pattern into which he is expected to fit. In short, what is a profession for the purposes of this study? Ambiguity has accrued to the term "profession" due to the development of systematic thought and ethics in a number of fields of endeavor. Some think that only medicine, law and the ministry should be accorded recognition as true professions; at the other extreme, some label as a professional almost anyone who wears a white collar to work. Alexander Carr-Saunders[5] has divided the term "professional" into five categories:

1. *Old established professions* are founded upon the study of a theoretical structure of a department of learning which is used in the practice of the art founded upon it, and the members of the vocation feel bound to follow a certain mode of behavior. Religion, law, medicine, higher education.

2. *New professions* have their own fundamental studies upon which their art is founded. Chemistry, engineering, natural and social sciences.

3. *Semi-professions* replace theoretical study of a field of learning by the acquisition of a precise technical skill. Nursing, optometry, pharmacy, social work.

4. *Would-be professions* are those where members aspire to professional status. Business and government.

5. *Marginal professions* are made up largely of those who perform technical assignments associated with professional assignments. Laboratory technicians.

For some people, the first of these five categories comprises the entire group of professions. This limited definition is little used in the social sciences today.

A more widely adopted definition is that used by the Bureau of the Census:[7] "Professional, technical and kindred workers." This classification includes all of the first four Carr-Saunders categories above and some of the fifth and it seems a realistic grouping in terms of occupational status in the United States today.

In the present study, one exception to the classification was made. Excluded from the group were "free professionals," persons who work as relatively independent agents. Doctors and lawyers are typical of this group. It was felt that since there were so few deaf persons engaged as independent agents and since their practices were so limited, their inclusion in the study group would destroy its homogeneity.* Hence, the study covers only those professional, technical and related occupations which are usually followed by an employee in a laboratory or an office.

CHOOSING THE RESPONDENTS

Selection Criteria

Besides the requirement that the respondents be engaged in a professional occupation, it was decided that this employment must have been of three years' duration. A minimum salary of $4,000 per year was another criterion; this was based upon the median salary ($4,040) for male deaf professional workers in the *Survey of Occupational Conditions Among the Deaf.*[2] Race and sex were

---

*Relative to the deaf population, there is a large number of deaf persons engaged in teaching and in the ministry, but with rare exceptions these professionals perform their services for deaf people only. In recent years there has been a small but significant move by deaf persons into other professional areas, such as vocational rehabilitation, social work and psychology. Here again dealings are, for the most part, with deaf clients. These groups do not fit the purpose of this study, which is concerned with the assimilation of deaf persons into a working environment that does not normally make allowances for a communication handicap.

not criteria. Despite diligent efforts, no Negro deaf professional workers other than teachers were discovered during the survey.

It was recognized that communication is the underlying problem in all phases of a deaf person's training, placement and advancement and that communication is a considerable factor in professional work. To assure that the communication situation would be more or less uniform, the group was limited to deaf persons working daily in offices or in laboratories with persons who hear. Hence, occupations like teaching and the ministry, in which deaf professionals work with and among other deaf persons, were excluded.

The study group was limited to persons deaf to the extent that their communication was visually oriented; that is, their reception of communication was through the eyes—reading written messages, reading the lips, observing gestures and clues or using the more formalized sign language and manual alphabet. This criterion of visual communication limited the group to those loosely described as profoundly or severely deaf. Persons who were able to receive communication through the ear were excluded. This does not mean, however, that the respondents had no residual hearing whatsoever. A few had sufficient residual hearing to aid them with lipreading, but none could use the telephone unaided.

Selection Procedure

Selection of the respondents was accomplished through a loosely controlled canvass of educators, social workers, clergymen and leaders among deaf groups.* In this initial canvass, precise definitions (of "professional" or "deaf," for example) were avoided so that the varied groups canvassed could respond with deaf workers in as wide a spectrum of employment as they wished. The actual selection would not be made until the lists received had been examined for job titles consistent with the aim, which was, at the time of the canvass, "deaf persons in professional, managerial or high-level technical employment." A card file of over 600 names and addresses was established from replies to this initial canvass. Examination of this file indicated

---

*Groups from whom names of possible respondents were sought: 74 residential schools for the deaf; 10 large public day schools for the deaf; 49 state directors of vocational rehabilitation; 44 hearing societies and leagues; 35 social clubs of the deaf; 63 individuals, including numerous leaders of organizations of the deaf; 9 ministers to deaf people.

that the desired group of 100 respondents probably could be obtained from among those classified as "professional, technical and kindred workers," a more homogeneous grouping than "professional, managerial and high-level technical."

From the card file thus established, there were selected 290 persons whose job titles were included in the Bureau of the Census's list of professional, technical and kindred workers.[4] A questionnaire was sent to these persons to test the preliminary classification. This questionnaire (see Appendix A) covered degree of ability to hear, occupational title and description, years employed and availability for interview. Replies to the questionnaire allowed further eliminations until the desired 100 respondents had been selected in accordance with criteria previously established: employment for three years or more in an occupation listed in the Census of Population under the category "professional, technical and kindred workers"; deafness of sufficient severity that the respondent's communication was necessarily visually oriented, i.e., received through reading, lipreading, the manual alphabet and/or the sign language; an age range of twenty-five to seventy years. Two of the 100 respondents originally selected were later eliminated when interviewers discovered that their hearing was better than replies to the questionnaire had seemed to indicate, and one was eliminated when it was discovered that his work was not of a professional nature. Ten others were lost in the interviewing process (explained below). The final group analyzed consisted of eighty-seven respondents.

A hearing colleague of each respondent was also interviewed briefly to discover the reactions of professional associates to the deaf person and the problems he had met at work. Selection of the colleague was left to the deaf respondent. Although it was recognized that such a method of selection might result in colleagues biased in favor of the respondent, the mechanics of selection by mail precluded any other method. A gain was the relatively long and close association of the colleague with the deaf person and hence a deeper understanding of the problems he had encountered.

INTERVIEWING

One of the most critical problems of the study was the manner of conducting the interviews. Since it was intended to tap the experience and opinions of the respondents it was necessary that the interview be relatively free. It was also intended to secure considerable factual and quantitative information and this required controlled questions. Asking open-end questions demands the highest sort of interviewing skill, but there existed no trained and experienced interviewers who were also fluent in the sign language and familiar with problems of oral communication with deaf persons. The latter two qualifications were considered essential for ease of communication and the rapport so necessary for a successful interview.

The two interviewers selected were children of deaf parents and hence were skilled in the use of the sign language and the manual alphabet. Both had had training in speech work. Neither had had prior training or experience in interviewing, but it was felt that communication ability was crucial and that, if interviewers were chosen for interviewing skill alone, a short course in the sign language would be completely ineffectual as a preparation for communication with the deaf respondents. The two interviewers selected received three weeks of training which included study and discussion of interviewing techniques, a thorough briefing in the use of the interview schedule and practice sessions with the investigator, the chief consultant and deaf persons who volunteered as interview subjects. The interviewers then conducted a dozen pretest interviews, chiefly in the Washington, DC, area. Their work was then reviewed and additional instruction was given as seemed necessary. The interviews were conducted during a period extending from May 1960 through February 1961.

The interview schedule* itself was a compromise of the two aims: factual detail and freely expressed opinions. Although many of the questions were highly structured, there were also numerous opportunities for, and probes to evoke free answers. In anticipation of the possibility that a few interviewees might lack receptive communication skills (the sign language, the manual alphabet or lipreading), the entire schedule was reproduced on cards, without the instructions intended for the interviewers. The cards proved useful in instances where lipreading failed on a question or two. For one respondent, the entire interview was conducted through the use of these cards.

---

*Copies of the schedules may be secured by writing to Alan B. Crammatte, Gallaudet College, Washington, DC, 20002.

A shorter questionnaire* (28 questions) was used with a colleague of each respondent.

A tape recorder was used to record the interviews. Initially, those respondents who were able to do so were encouraged to speak their replies for the tape recorder. Problems of distortion of speech errors soon appeared, resulting in the loss of ten interviews because significant portions of the replies were unintelligible. As experience of the interviewers increased, a method of interviewing was devised whereby the interviewer repeated the replies of the respondents into the microphone regardless of whether the replies were spoken or delivered in the sign language. Recording the interviews which were conducted in the sign language required a great facility in this means of communication on the part of the interviewers. They found it necessary to translate the gestures of the sign language immediately into words and to speak them into the microphone while at the same time preparing to ask the next question.

The location of the interviews was necessarily determined by the interviewees, generally at their place of employment. A well-lighted room was highly desirable because of the visual nature of the communication and quietness was needed for good recording fidelity. This ideal of a quiet, well-lighted room was not always achieved. One interview was conducted in the stacks of a library; one colleague served as a registrar of voters while being interviewed, with side remarks duly recorded; one recording had for a background noise the crying of the respondent's baby. A direct-current electric circuit blew out the tape recorder once, fortunately in the city where it had been manufactured. Yet these difficulties can be said to have been slight compared with those of coping with tight flying schedules (two lengthy interviews one day and a 9 AM appointment in a distant city the next) and dragging a clutter of heavy equipment from one end of a strange city to the other. The physical strain upon the interviewers was great. A much more leisurely travel plan is recommended for future interviewing trips.

THE COLLEAGUES

Each respondent was asked to name a colleague who would consent to a short interview to give a co-worker's view of the deaf man's problems and abilities. Thought was given to specifying the type of colleague, but it was concluded that the varied situations from which they would be recruited precluded any criteria other than close association with the respondent. A majority (forty-five) of the colleagues had known the respondents four years or less; 29 per cent had been acquainted with the respondent ten years or more. Almost three-fourths of the colleagues ranked above the respondent in the hierarchy of the firm, many being the respondent's direct supervisor; fifteen were of the same rank and six ranked lower. Actual positions of the colleagues ranged from firm presidents to secretaries; twenty-four (28 per cent) were division chiefs or of higher rank, seven of these being heads of firms; forty-four were supervisory, from branch chiefs to group leaders; fourteen were professional staff workers and three clerks. All evinced considerable interest in the problems of fitting a deaf man into a normally oral environment. Some broached their own management problems in relation to the respondent.

ACKNOWLEDGMENTS

THIS PUBLICATION is the final report of a research project sponsored by Gallaudet College and supported by a grant from the Vocational Rehabilitation Administration.

The study was conceived during correspondence and discussion between the author and Dr. Ben M. Schowe, former labor economist at the Firestone Tire and Rubber Company. He kept the idea alive until the grant was sought and participated actively in the formulation of plans once the study was begun.

Chief among those aiding in the execution of the project was Stanley K. Bigman, who lent his considerable talents to the design of the study and especially to the drafting of the extensive interview schedules.

In the gathering of the data, the interviewers played a key role and a very difficult one; they not only interviewed but simultaneously translated the respondents' sign language into speech for the tape recorder, a rare skill. Besides their interviewing duties, Mrs. Carol Isaacson Pace and Mr. Louie J. Fant, Jr., were of great help with voluntary advice and assistance in other matters.

Mrs. Dorothy S. Miles served far above and beyond her duties as secretary, contributing her editorial skills to the drafting of the report. The director's family also helped in numerous ways during the project, not the least of which was patience during the agonies of composition; his wife was especially helpful in the final editing of the manuscript.

Boyce R. Williams, Consultant on the Deaf and the Hard-of-Hearing, Vocational Rehabilitation Administration, was the inspiration for the project. Without his example of dedicated service and his loyal patience, the project might never have been accomplished.

ALAN B. CRAMMATTE
Project Director

CONTENTS

Deaf Persons
in
Professional Employment

Chapter I

THE CHARACTERISTICS OF A PROFESSIONAL WORKER

THERE IS LITTLE DOUBT that, among the deaf populace, the respondents in this study form something of an elite. Their being selected by various leaders in matters concerning education and welfare of deaf people attests to the stature of their positions. They rank above most other deaf people in the material measures of success: high-status employment, challenging work, comfortable salaries, better homes and other material rewards. The community of deaf people and those who serve them look upon the respondents as vocationally outstanding.

A question arises as to whether this assessment of the position of the respondents is valid. How do they compare with the general concept of a professional person? Based on the selection criteria, their job titles and descriptions correspond to the Bureau of the Census grouping, "professional, technical and kindred," but do they have other attributes generally ascribed to professional workers?

A capsule description of the professional worker was given by Miller and Form[11] in these words:

> The typical professional worker is . . . born unto an upper middle- or upper-class family. His father is a business proprietor or manager. . . . He encourages his son to plan on going to college . . . the son enrolls in a professional curriculum and begins his specialized training . . . upon completion of his professional schooling he moves directly into his professional career without floundering. During his first four years out of college he moves twice as he seeks a "good" firm or a "good" location for his professional practice. He finds what he wants for a permanent location and settles down in an urban community. . . . He receives an income which permits him to live above the comfort level. . . . He is, in fact, one of the most stable workers, occupationally, of any group in the community. He has high prestige and is widely sought as a leader in community organizations.

A generalized description formulated by the authors from various studies, the above quotation provides a reasonable model for a broad estimate of these respondents as professional people.

If the occupational rank of the father can be used as the criterion of social status of the respondents' families, then it may be said that they represent largely upper middle- and upper-class families. Of the fathers of the eighty-seven respondents, forty-six (53 per cent) were engaged in professional or non-farm managerial pursuits during most of the respondents' childhood. Twenty-nine fathers (33 per cent) were in clerical and sales positions or in the skilled crafts. Only five were relatively unskilled workers or unemployed, as is shown in Table 1.

TABLE 1

OCCUPATIONAL STATUS OF RESPONDENTS' FATHERS

Professional and technical workers	28
Proprietors, managers and officials (farm)	4
Proprietors, managers and officials (non-farm)	18
Clerical, sales and kindred workers	4
Craftsmen, foremen and kindred workers	25
Laborers, operatives and service workers	4
Other	2*
Unemployed	1
No reply	1
Total	87

*Died when respondents were children.

Of the eighty-seven respondents, sixty-one (70 per cent) had been graduated from college, according to Table 2. This percentage exceeds the proportion of respondents in the *Survey of Occupational Conditions*[2] who had attended college at all (67 per cent). Indeed, the present respondents who had attended college at all comprised eighty-two (94 per cent of the group). The respondents, of course, are a select grouping whereas the *Survey* is the only available representation of the general deaf population.

Almost half of the respondents had undertaken graduate study. Seventeen had earned the master's degree and five the doctorate. Of those who did no graduate study, only seventeen were below age thirty-five, making it seem unlikely that many more of these respondents would seek degrees beyond the bachelor's.

TABLE 2

HIGHEST EDUCATIONAL LEVEL ATTAINED BY RESPONDENTS

Educational Level Completed	Number	Per Cent
High school graduate	5	6
Some college study	21	24
Bachelor's degree	22	25
Some graduate study	17	20
Master's degree	17	20
Doctor's degree	5	6
Total	87	101*

*Adds to 101 per cent because of rounding.

Not all the respondents had "enrolled in a professional curriculum," as is shown in Table 3. Five had not gone to college. Of the twenty-one who had attended but had not been graduated from college, nine had not chosen a major field. Four were graduated from a liberal arts program without a major. A good many of those who reported having had a major in chemistry, mathematics or library science had been graduated from Gallaudet College, the only college for deaf students, where, until the 1950s, these three subjects received some emphasis but where there was no accredited program of majors in any field. However, thirty-nine (45 per cent) of the respondents went on to graduate study which probably offered a professional cur-

TABLE 3

RESPONDENTS' MAJOR FIELDS OF CONCENTRATION DURING UNDERGRADUATE YEARS AND NUMBER NOW IN THE SAME OR RELATED OCCUPATIONS

	Respondents	
Major Fields of Concentration During Undergraduate Years	Number	In Same or Related Occupations
Sciences (including engineering)	41	41
Economics and business administration	6	3
Mathematics and statistics	5	5
English	3	2
Library science	2	2
Other	3*	3
Liberal arts	13	
No college	5	
No reply	9	
Total	87	56

*Includes one respondent each in agriculture, architecture and mechanical arts.

riculum. Almost half of the respondents (forty-one) had studied one of the sciences as a major field.

Most of the respondents may be said to have "moved into their professional careers without floundering," even though the securing of the first job may have been difficult. Of the sixty who said they had majored in a definite field of concentration, fifty-six were engaged in that field of work at the time of the interview. One or more of the thirteen liberal arts students were employed in each of the eight occupational categories used in this report: art and architecture, business, chemistry, engineering, library work and museum work, mathematics and statistics, other sciences and miscellaneous.†

The respondents seemed to have secured employment in "good" companies. The roster of employers included many business firms and research centers of wide repute.* The chief employer was the United States Government; nineteen agencies of the government employed twenty-four of the respondents.

Almost all of the respondents lived in urban areas.‡

The respondents, in the main, earned incomes at or above the comfort level, as may be seen in Table 4. The median income from salary or wages of the group was $7,615 per year, almost $400 greater than the median income of professional workers in the United States labor force in 1960[15] (including teachers, who are excluded in the respondent group).

It may be assumed that the respondents had prestige to some degree or they would not have been discovered in a canvass such as was used. They were not, however, leaders in their communities as was Miller and Form's "typical" professional worker. The respondents cannot be called active joiners. Almost half the group belonged to only two organizations of the deaf or less; more than half (51 per

---

†Listed in detail in Table 42.
*See Appendix C for a complete listing.
‡The significance of this fact is obscure. It could have been caused by the location in urban areas of large firms with professional opportunities. It could, on the other hand, result from a tendency of deaf persons to gather in large cities. It could also be, to an extent, bias in the selection of respondents. Since a great majority of the prospective respondents were found to live in urban areas, some individuals in isolated places were not included in the group to be interviewed. Concentrating on respondents in urban areas saved travel and time. The group was not intended to be a sample or representative geographically.

cent) belonged to only one community (not restricted to deaf members) organization or none. Few of the respondents were very active in those organizations which they did join.

The respondents were stable employees. More than half of them had not changed employers more than once in their entire careers; indeed, twenty-four had been with one employer all their working lives. Only twenty-seven had changed jobs more than twice as compared to Miller and Form's model who moved twice during his first four years out of college.*

The great majority of the respondents were men (seventy-nine of the eighty-seven). In age (shown in Table 4) the respondents seemed slightly older than the professional persons in the general population of the United States, probably due to longer than average periods of educational preparation and job searching.

TABLE 4

AGE: RESPONDENTS AND THE PROFESSIONAL POPULATION OF THE UNITED STATES AGE 25 AND OVER

Age	Respondents		Professional Workers in US Population[16]
	Number	Per Cent	Per Cent
25 to 34	21	24	31.6
35 to 44	25	29	28.2
45 to 54	27	31	22.6
55 to 64	10	11	13.1
65 and over	4	5	4.5
Total	87	100	100.0

It can be said that the respondents, on the whole, did fit well the description of the average professional person as drawn by Miller and Form. The only exception was in the area of community leadership. For the purposes of this study, it may be assumed that the demands of coping with their occupations despite communication handicaps must have served to limit the respondents' participation in community affairs, but the finding presents interesting possibilities for further research and analysis.

---

*Chapter VII, "Occupational Mobility," examines this characteristic more thoroughly.

Chapter II

COMMUNICATION

COMMUNICATION is an ever-present, all-pervasive problem for any deaf person. Even before a deaf baby knows anything about expressing himself, his life pattern may be deeply affected by the emotional reaction of his parents to the fact that their child is handicapped. Subsequent parent-child relationships also may be made difficult by communication problems. A deaf person's education is conditioned by the need to find compensation for the inability to hear. The effect may range from the profound interference with language acquisition caused by early deafness to the excessive time allotted to various special instruction courses in the curriculum. A deaf person's training opportunities, occupational selection, employment, advancement, recreation, community participation and even his marital selection and happiness may be affected by the handicap. For the deaf professional person the pervasive nature of the communication problem is extended further by the need to express and receive ideas clearly as a part of his work.*

His problems may be further complicated by the attitudes which the communication difficulty may engender in others. Unfamiliar with the problems of deafness, hearing persons often do not listen patiently or they may exaggerate their speech in a mistaken effort to make understanding easier for the deaf person. Language difficulties they may interpret as lack of intelligence. Corollary to such attitudes is the uneasy question, "Will he fit into our organization?" or excessive enthusiasm for the deaf person who does fit.

The child born profoundly deaf or deafened very early in life

---

*This is not to say that the deaf adult is in a continuous dilemma about how to convey his thoughts or to receive those of others. He has, through training and experience, acquired methods of communication which serve him more or less satisfactorily. These skills he uses instinctively, automatically employing the method that fits the situation best. Likewise, many deaf persons may build up inner defenses to such embarrassment and frustrations as may occur because of their deafness.

receives none of the oral stimuli which normally form the basis for development of speech. Such a child's approach to learning to talk must be visual and tactile. Control of sound must be taught where no concept of sound exists. Proper manipulation of the speech organs is taught by illustration, example and endless repetition.

Lipreading is a part of the speech-learning process as well as a difficult skill in itself. The formations of the speech organs observed by a deaf child in learning to talk are basically those which must be observed in reading the lips, although individual variations complicate the process. Additionally, even the competent speech reader must be able to synthesize a complete meaning from sketchy word clues, for no lip-reader reads *every* word the speaker says. Anticipation of the direction of the conversation and perception of clues from gestures and facial expressions are other skills needed for lipreading.

The laborious nature of learning oral communication cannot be exaggerated; perfection is practically never achieved, although results are spectacular in any case. These are factors to consider when examining the data concerning communication by deaf persons.

Communication, of course, is not solely a matter of speech and hearing. Writing, for example, is a widely used supplement to speech. With a deaf person, writing is often more than a supplement; sometimes it may serve as a complete substitute for oral communication. Even in this respect, the child deafened early is handicapped. His vocabulary must be wholly taught to him; none of it can be picked up subconsciously from what is heard. His acquisition of language is highly structured and his reception of ideas is often disjointed (due to the elisions of speech reading and the ideographic syntax of the sign language). Because of these factors, the deaf adult's vocabulary may be limited and his writing more or less stilted.

Perhaps the most frequently used means of communication by deaf people among themselves is with the hands. Manual communication takes two forms: manual spelling and the sign language. The former consists of a series of finger formations which indicate the letters of the alphabet and the numbers. In the United States the letters are formed with one hand; in Great Britain they are made with both hands. The general effect is similar—something that amounts to writing in the air. The manual alphabet can be learned in a matter of minutes.

The sign language is somewhat more complicated. As a symbol system which replaces ordinary speech, it consists of hand formations and motions which convey ideas. It is a form of pantomime; for example, one says "drink" by raising to the mouth a hand formed as a cup. The gestures, however, may be said to be much more formalized than the sort of pantomime with which many hearing people supplement their speech. The number of signs, or ideographs, is relatively limited when we consider the number of words in the dictionary. It is incorrect, however, to assume that the sign language is therefore crude and limited in expression. Emphasis through speed or strength of the signs and with facial expression allows communication of a multitude of ideas in a manner as dramatic, or as precise, as may be desired. In the hands of a master the sign language can be a sharp and powerful tool for communication.

There is another form of manual communication—informal gestures and spur of the moment pantomime—that is used to a considerable extent by friends and co-workers with deaf persons. These gestures are considerably different from the highly stylized sign language. In this report, the term "manual communication" is used generically to mean all symbolization with the hands. However, it is well to assume that when the subject is that of communication between hearing persons and deaf persons, "manual" will usually refer to the informal gestures just described.

MEANS OF COMMUNICATION MOST FREQUENTLY USED AT WORK

By what means did the respondents communicate with their business associates who hear? During the interview respondents were given a card listing "writing, speech, manual spelling, sign language, natural gestures and other (specify)." They were then asked, "Which of these methods do you use the most when you communicate *to* hearing persons at work?" They were also asked, "Which of these methods do you use the most when hearing persons communicate to *you?*" As may be seen from the phrasing of the two questions, the first was intended to elicit methods of expressive communication (how the respondent communicated to others) and the second was meant to bring out methods of receptive communication (how the respondent received communication from others). Similar questions were asked about communication with hearing persons off the job and with deaf people on and off the job. Informal queries sought the next most frequent means of communication and, where possible, the third, so that a ranking* of the means of communication used by each respondent was secured. The results for communication with hearing persons at work are shown in Table 5.

TABLE 5

MEANS OF COMMUNICATION MOST FREQUENTLY USED WITH HEARING PERSONS AT WORK, EXPRESSIVE AND RECEPTIVE, BY RANK OF CHOICE*

Means of Communication	Expressive		Receptive	
	First Choice Per Cent	Second Choice Per Cent	First Choice Per Cent	Second Choice Per Cent
Oral	63	21	55	29
Written	35	39	40	39
Manual	2	15	5	20
No answer		25		13
Total	100	100	100	101
(Number)	(87)	(87)	(87)	(87)

*Only 18 respondents registered a third choice for expressive communication; of these, 15 per cent of all the respondents used manual and 5 per cent oral means. Third choices for receptive communication were: manual, 21 per cent; oral, 9 per cent, and written, 2 per cent.

Almost two-thirds of the respondents made speech their most frequently used means of expressive communication with business associates who hear. A somewhat smaller proportion, 55 per cent, made lipreading their choice for receptive communication.

Perhaps the most significant fact in Table 5, however, is that seventy-three of the eighty-seven respondents (84 per cent) used oral communication as a first or second most frequent means. If the third most frequent means were to be included, it could be said that 90 per cent of the respondents used speech, and 93 per cent, lipreading to some extent.

Very few respondents used manual communication with hearing

---

*Ranking was chosen in preference to the use of percentages because the choice was too subjective and variable to be expressed by a medium implying precision, as would percentages.

business associates. The low frequency may probably be attributed to lack of skill in the sign language among the associates rather than among the respondents. Table 7 shows that over 80 per cent of the respondents used manual means with other deaf persons.

Examination of the second choices in relation to the first choices reveals, as might be expected, that a large number of the respondents who most frequently used oral means used writing as the alternative. Similarly, when writing was the most frequently used means, the oral means was the alternative. A large number (nineteen out of fifty-five), who used speech for expressive communication recorded no second most frequent means, indicating, it may be assumed, that no other was needed. Fewer respondents (ten out of forty-nine) were able to rely entirely on oral means for receptive communication.

When the data on methods of expressive communication were distributed by methods of receptive communication used at work, the respondents indicated similar frequencies of oral and non-oral communication. Of those who used speech most frequently, 79 per cent used lipreading for receptive communication; of those who communicated by writing or by manual means, a slightly larger percentage (eighty-four) used the same means for reception.

A few of the respondents volunteered comments on problems in using the oral means of communication. Several specified that with close acquaintances speech and lipreading were used, but with strangers writing was employed first and then speech. Control of voice volume is always a problem and a respondent said, "I often don't realize how much noise is going around. So then they must ask me to repeat." Another respondent combined problems of speech and lipreading: "I must know them very well before I can talk. If I don't know them and they find out that I am deaf (from imperfections of speech), they try too hard to make me understand and I can't understand a word they say."

One hypothesis of this study is that professional employment requires communication skills and that deaf persons in professional occupations must have higher proficiency in, and more variety of, communication skills than the average deaf person. The nearest approximation to the average deaf person is found in the statistics of the Bigman-Lunde *Survey of Occupational Conditions Among the*

Deaf.[2] Unfortunately, the survey did not rank the methods of communication by frequency of use; since such information was unavailable, the percentages of total respondents who used each method were calculated. Also, the survey did not differentiate between expressive and receptive communication. These deficiencies make comparison with present data* somewhat difficult. However, comparison is possible if the first, second and third ranking choices of the present respondents are considered as those choices which they would have checked on the *Survey of Occupational Conditions* questionnaire. It is likewise necessary to accept an average of frequencies in expressive and receptive written communication as reported here to be equivalent to the "writing" item, which in the Bigman-Lunde report included both expressive and receptive writing. Using the Bigman-Lunde terminology, the data may be presented as in Table 6.

In comparison with the respondents in the *Survey of Occupational Conditions,* the respondents in this study reported more communication skills at their command, the percentages being greater in every

TABLE 6

METHODS OF COMMUNICATION USED WITH HEARING
PERSONS AT WORK*

Means of Communication	Respondents[†] Per Cent	Respondents in The Survey of Occupational Conditions Among the Deaf[2]	
		Non-Teaching[§] *Professionals Per Cent*	*Total Respondents Per Cent*
Writing	77	59.4	67.9
Talking	90	62.3	36.4
Lipreading	93	58.6	33.5
Sign language	32	15.5	18.9
Finger spelling		24.3	16.8
Not reported	19	unk.	3.0
Total Respondents	(87)[‡]	(239)[‡]	(7920)[‡]

*Respondents and Respondents in *The Survey of Occupational Conditions Among the Deaf*: total and professional, technical and kindred workers.

†Data were derived from Table 5.

‡Columns add to more than 100 per cent because of multiple answers.

§Teachers in schools for the deaf were eliminated from the column "Non-Teaching Professionals" because their frequent use of manual communication in their work made the figures not comparable with those of the respondents.

*Data are derived from Table 5.

category except the sign language. The difference between the present respondents and all respondents in the *Survey* for talking and for lipreading (93 and 33.5 per cent) are especially remarkable.

Means of communication with deaf persons off the job are analyzed in Table 7 in relation to the means used with hearing associates at work.

TABLE 7

MEANS OF COMMUNICATION USED MOST FREQUENTLY WITH HEARING PERSONS AT WORK, BY THAT USED WITH DEAF PERSONS OFF THE JOB

Means of Communication Used with Hearing Persons at Work	*Means of Communication With Deaf Persons off the Job*				
	Total	*Oral*	*Written*	*Manual*	*No Deaf Friends*
Expressive:					
Oral	55	15	1	32	7
Written	30	2	1	27	—
Manual	2	—	—	2	—
Total	87	17	2	61	7
Receptive:					
Oral	48	14	1	28	5
Written	35	2	1	30	2
Manual	4	—	—	4	—
Total	87	16	2	62	7

As might be expected, manual means predominated in communication of the respondents among deaf people. About 75 per cent of the respondents used manual means of communication the most frequently. Seventeen respondents (20 per cent) used speech most frequently, but ten of them also used manual means the next most frequently; that is, they communicated orally with some deaf persons and used the sign language and manual alphabet with others. Hence, it can be said that over 80 per cent of the respondents were able to use a manual symbol system in communicating with other deaf persons. As might be expected, those who communicated with deaf persons orally and those who had no deaf friends were found among those who communicated most frequently with hearing business associates by oral means. Analysis of communication with deaf persons at work was not attempted because fifty-three of the eighty-seven respondents had no deaf co-workers. Of the thirty-four remaining, twenty-eight used manual communication with deaf co-workers.

PREFERRED MEANS OF COMMUNICATION
WITH BUSINESS ASSOCIATES

In planning the study, a question arose as to whether deaf persons situated as were the respondents use the means of communication which they indicate to be the most frequent because their environment demands it or because they prefer that means. Respondents were asked, "With what means of communication do you feel the most comfortable when you are communicating *to* hearing business associates?" Also they were asked, "With that means of communication do you feel the most comfortable when hearing business associates communicate to *you?*"

In tabulating the information derived from these questions, two mixed classes were used. One, "oral and written," included those respondents who indicated that they generally preferred oral communication but also used writing for complex technical discussion, where clarity is essential, or with strangers, whose speech might be unfamiliar. In the "written and oral" classification the emphasis was reversed; the respondents preferred writing for most conversations but also liked speech where it was possible—in greetings, yes-or-no responses and other brief communications. The mixed classifications were not used in coding when respondents had minimized their second preference. Where suitable in cross tabulations, these mixed replies were added to the class represented by the first word in the title. The order of tabulation in Table 8 shows the relationship.

The reasons for the replies described as mixed were best stated by one respondent who indicated a preference for interpretation of others' speech into the sign language: ". . . you may get the general

TABLE 8
PREFERRED MEANS OF COMMUNICATION WITH HEARING
BUSINESS ASSOCIATES, EXPRESSIVE AND RECEPTIVE

Preferred Means of Communication	Expressive		Receptive	
	Number	Per Cent	Number	Per Cent
Oral	48	55	20	23
Oral and written	5	6	15	17
Written	26	30	40	46
Written and oral	5	6	5	6
Manual	3	3	4	5
No answer	—	—	3	3
Total	87	100	87	100

gist or flow of a conversation (through lipreading)—enough of the key words—but it's very easy to put the wrong slant on it without all of the details and they come through on the manual interpretation." The statement also applies to writing as regards accuracy of reception.

Speech was the preferred means of expressive communication for 55 per cent of the respondents, but only 23 per cent entirely preferred lipreading for reception. If the mixed replies are included, the percentages are 61 and 40, respectively. The inference from these data would seem to be that lipreading was more difficult or less satisfying for the respondents, on the whole, than their use of speech. Also, some of the respondents were deafened in later youth and thus retained proficiency in speech but did not acquire proficiency in lipreading.

A variety of answers were received to probes for reasons for preferences. These were classified by the aspects of the communication situation which they described. The answer, "competence," referred to the respondents' estimates of their ability to speak or read lips. With those deafened early in life, it was expressed by such remarks as "I am able," "I am trained to it," "I ask no favors," "I never used the sign language in my growing years." Competence was expressed by those deafened in their teens by "Speech . . . used it as a child. Much easier" or "Speech by associates . . . what other method could they use?" "Clarity" included such remarks as "to prevent misunderstanding," "for accuracy." "Suitability" was used to cover all of those who gave mixed replies; they suited the method to the situation. "Accommodation" referred to those who said, in effect, what one respondent said: "They feel better if you communicate with them in a way to which they are accustomed." "Embarrassment" included such replies as: "Speech . . . because that's normal I don't like segregation to be pointed out" and "Writing (for reception) . . . I get embarrassed very easily when I am misunderstood."

From Table 9 it can be seen that competence was the chief reason expressed by those who preferred to communicate orally. Clarity was the leading reason of those who preferred to write. These views applied to both expressive and receptive communication.

Examination of the two dominant reasons for communication pref-

TABLE 9
PREFERRED MEANS OF COMMUNICATION, BY REASONS FOR PREFERENCE

Preferred Means of Communication	Total	Competence	Clarity	Suitability	Speed	Accommodation	Embarrassment	No answer
Expressive:								
Oral	48	32	2	—	7	5	1	1
Oral and written	5	—	—	5	—	—	—	—
Written	26	—	24	—	2	—	—	—
Written and oral	5	—	—	5	—	—	—	—
Manual	3	1	1	—	1	—	—	—
Total	87	33	27	10	10	5	1	1
Receptive:								
Oral	20	12	—	—	2	4	1	1
Oral and written	15	—	—	15	—	—	—	—
Written	40	—	34	—	3	1	—	2
Written and oral	5	—	—	5	—	—	—	—
Manual	4	2	1	—	—	—	—	1
No answer	3	—	—	—	—	—	—	3
Total	87	14	35	20	5	5	1	7

erences, in relation to age when deafness occurred, indicates that age of occurrence is a factor in the preference frequencies.

The very wide differences in proportions for expressive and receptive communication appear to indicate that those who had lost their hearing at an age when some oral communication skills had been acquired were able to speak well and found it a natural means but did not achieve a like competence in lipreading, whereas those deafened at an age under six years who considered themselves competent in speech generally had a like confidence in their lipreading ability. Those who preferred writing because of clarity could be looked upon as the reverse side of this coin.

TABLE 10
REASONS FOR PREFERRED MEANS OF COMMUNICATION, BY AGE WHEN DEAFNESS OCCURRED

Age When Deafness Occurred	Reasons for Preferred Means of Communication			
	Oral—Competence*		Written—Clarity*	
	Expressive	Receptive	Expressive	Receptive
Under 6 years	15	9	20	22
Over 6 years	17	3	4	12
Total	32	12	24	34

*Figures taken from these categories of Table 9.

It must be remembered, of course, that competence is a relative term and that very likely the degree of speech competence of those deafened at an early age may be comparable to that of the deaf-born respondent who said:

> If I am on the street talking to a stranger, about 55 per cent of them suspect I am German because of my accent and inflection and about 40 per cent of them will think I am French, and the other 5 per cent will think I am Dutch or Spanish or Italian because of the speech.

His attitude about this situation is of value here, too:

> *Interviewer:* Did that create problems for you?
> *Respondent:* No. It amused me. I realized that I could not speak as naturally as a hearing person, but as long as I made myself understood, that was important.

Remarks of the respondents illuminate some of the subtler problems of expressive communication by deaf persons:

> I realized I (would) have to communicate mostly with normal hearing people, so I forced myself to use speech as much as possible.

> When they hear me (talk), they become dubious of my ability. It gives them the wrong impression. They kind of hesitate.

Some attributed their use of speech to their training:

> ... and because I went to a school for the deaf where they emphasized the oral method.

Similar revelations were made about reception. Some preferred non-oral means because

> It's less nerve-wracking than to watch them all the time, reading the lips.

The mixed replies (oral-written and written-oral) frequently mentioned the difficulty of reading the lips of a stranger or of the deaf person's *bete noire,* the man with a walrus moustache. One respondent said, "Lipreading is largely guesswork and I prefer them to write to me." On the other hand, some objected to the very idea of the pencil-and-pad method of conversing:

> I am not one of those deaf people who always have a pad and pencil around.

> I do not like for anybody to communicate to me by writing on a piece of paper.

Preferences and means actually used are quite similar in frequency as regards expressive communication, but it is obvious from the figures below that a considerable proportion of the respondents who used oral means for receptive communication would have preferred other means.

TABLE 11

MEANS OF COMMUNICATION USED OR PREFERRED, BY THAT USED MOST FREQUENTLY AT WORK

| Means of Communication Used Most Frequently at Work | Means of Communication | | | |
| | Expressive | | Receptive | |
	Used Per Cent	Preferred Per Cent	Used Per Cent	Preferred Per Cent
Oral	63	61	55	41
Non-oral	37	39	45	56
Total	100	100	100	97*

*Does not add to 100 per cent because one respondent did not reply.

SPEECH SKILLS

A pertinent question is whether the use of, and preference for, various means of communication were related to the respondents' skills in speech and lipreading. There were, however, no feasible objective tests of these skills. A measurement of lipreading ability might have been the Utley test,[17] but it would have burdened the interviewer with motion picture projection equipment in addition to notebook, tape recorder, interview cards and other paraphernalia. There are no objective tests of speech possible without extensive control of environment. Under these circumstances, the method of rating the respondents on their skills in speech and lipreading was necessarily subjective and rather crude.

A set of scaled questions was adopted to secure a rough evaluation of the respondent's skill in speech and in lipreading from him and from his colleague. The respondent was given a card on which were typed four statements about the quality of his speech and he was asked, "Which of these describes best how well your hearing business associates seem to understand your speech in your *usual* working environment?" The statements on the card read as follows:

1. They understand practically everything I say.
2. They understand almost everything I say, but must listen carefully.

3. They understand only a word or two now and then.

4. None of these (what?).

Similarly, respondents were asked to evaluate their lipreading ability in terms of the following statements:

1. I understand almost everything they say, no matter how they say it.

2. I understand a short conversation, when it is spoken carefully.

3. I understand only short, simple sentences, spoken very carefully.

4. I understand only a word or two now and then.

The same approach was used for evaluation by colleagues except that the sentences on the cards were worded to fit that situation. For example, the first statement about speech read, "I understand practically everything he (the respondent) says," and the first one about lipreading read, "He understands almost everything I say, no matter how I say it." Thus the rough evaluation by the two persons was made on scaling systems as nearly alike as possible.

Table 12 shows how the respondents were rated on speech skills by themselves and by their colleagues.

Over two-fifths of the respondents felt that practically all their speech was understandable; one-third felt that almost everything they said was understood if the listener took care. They were less sanguine about their lipreading skill. Only 21 per cent understood almost everything said to them; slightly more than a third of them understood only short, simple sentences or a word or two now and then.

It is evident that colleagues rated the respondents more highly in speech and lipreading than did the respondents themselves. Especially was this true in lipreading, for which the colleagues placed 43 per cent of the respondents at the top, whereas only 21 per cent of the respondents so rated themselves.

In coding the interviews, these ratings by respondent and by colleague were compared for each individual. The colleague was found to have rated the respondent higher than the respondent had rated himself in twenty out of eighty-six cases for speech and in thirty-three out of eighty cases for lipreading. In only nine cases for speech and ten for lipreading did the colleague rate the respondent lower than the respondent did himself.

TABLE 12
SPEECH SKILLS, EXPRESSIVE AND RECEPTIVE, AS PERCEIVED BY RESPONDENTS AND BY THEIR COLLEAGUES

Speech Skills	Perceived by Respondent		Perceived by Colleague	
Speech:	Number	Per Cent	Number	Per Cent
Associates understood:				
Practically all said	37	43	48	55
Almost everything, with care	29	33	22	25
Occasional word or two	15	17	10	11
Respondent never spoke	3	3	6	7
Other	2*	2		
No answer	1	1	1†	1
Total	87	99	87	99
Lipreading:				
Respondent understood:				
Almost everything said	18	21	37	43
Short conversation	37	43	24	28
Short, simple sentences	19	22	13	15
Occasional word or two	11	13	3	3
Colleague never spoke to respondent			3	3
No answer	2	2	7†	8
Total	87	101	87	100

*Understanding varied with length of acquaintance.
†One had no colleague interview.

It is difficult to ascribe any one reason for this tendency of colleagues to rate respondents higher. Among the many variables to confuse the issue are exaggerated admiration by colleagues for a skill they may not fully understand, tendency to upgrade a co-worker, divergent interpretation of the rating statements and modesty of the respondents. The higher rating by colleagues occurred much more frequently in evaluating lipreading, possibly because they were guessing at how much the respondent actually had understood, whereas in evaluating the respondent's speech they knew exactly what communication they had understood. However, it seems safe to conclude that these colleagues did, as a rule, consider the respondents to be better oral communicators than the respondents did themselves. From that conclusion it might be inferred that deaf persons could take a more confident view of their skills—or at least of the reception given to their skills by their companions who hear.

There is, however, a qualification to be made to the high ratings of these respondents by colleagues. The colleagues were persons of long acquaintance with the deaf respondents, and hence they were more familiar with the peculiarities of the respondents' speech and probably more tolerant of the repetitions or gaps in understanding that occurred in communicating through lipreading. Some colleagues qualified their ratings with "This is for people who work closely with him." Other descriptions by these colleagues of the communication process with a deaf person are revealing:

> I understand practically everything he says through long familiarity; strangers have a little more difficulty.

> It takes some practice before you get accustomed to understanding him and making yourself understood. But after a short time things go rather well, I think.

> He forms words and makes a sound and some of his sounds are different . . . At the beginning you have difficulty understanding, but when you familiarize yourself with his sounds—when you get to know him—it's a matter of the more you live with him or work with him the better you understand him.

Some colleagues showed real comprehension of technical problems of lipreading. For instance, providing a clue:

> When you hit him cold, it's hard for him to understand, but if you lead up to it or provide a key word, it's easier.

The importance of a clear, full view:

> Always realizing that he is deaf and in talking to him being sure that he can always see your mouth moving.

The danger of overcareful, exaggerated pronunciation:

> If one goes to great pains to carefully form words, he has more difficulty than if one just follows the normal approach for conversation.

Did skill in speech and in lipreading correlate with the means of communication these respondents used at work? If so, it would be expected that of those respondents who rated themselves at the top of the scale of skills, a large proportion would use speech at work, with the proportion declining as the rating of skill declined. Table 13 bears out this assumption:

Similar proportions existed in relation to speech skills and preferred means of communication.

TABLE 13

SPEECH SKILLS BY MEANS OF COMMUNICATION MOST
FREQUENTLY USED WITH HEARING PERSONS AT WORK

Speech Skills	Means of Communication Most Frequently Used at Work		
	Total	*Oral*	*Non-Oral*
Speech:			
Practically all said	37	32	5
Almost everything	29	19	10
Occasional word or two	15	1	14
Never spoke	3	1	2
Other	3	2*	1†
Total	87	55	32
Lipreading:			
Almost everything said	18	16	2
Short conversation	37	27	10
Short, simple sentences	19	4	15
Occasional word or two	11	—	11
Never spoke to respondent	2	1	1
Total	87	48	39

*Understanding varied with length of acquaintance.
†No colleague.

AGE OF OCCURRENCE OF DEAFNESS

One of the early questions asked in the assessment of a deaf child's learning potential is the age when deafness occurred. This factor has far-reaching effects on all of the learning process and especially on the acquisition of speech. This situation exists because of the pattern of speech maturation and acquisition of vocabulary. A very young baby is basically a noisemaker; he responds to discomfort with wails, to pleasant sensation with coos and gurgles. At the age of two or three years he begins to realize, from the constant association of what he hears with what occurs thereafter, that the different noises he experiences bring different results. By the time he is six years old and ready for school, he has acquired, in the main subconsciously, the ability to communicate in more or less ordered sentences. His vocabulary and comprehension of the nuances of vocal communication continue to grow until, by his early teens, he possesses a wide-ranging and flexible tool of communication. Along with this development of speech and hearing, there occurs a similar growth in language comprehension, largely subconscious in early years but ordered and taught after he enters school.

If a child becomes deaf, this pattern of growth is disturbed. The results are serious in inverse proportion to the age at which deafness occurs because the earlier the occurrence of deafness the weaker the foundation for learning speech and language. If deafness occurs before the age of three years or so, the task will be the tedious one of being taught* the very concept of speech, each elementary sound and practically each combination of sounds. If hearing loss occurs between the ages of three and six the concept of speech as a mode of communication probably has been established and some vocabulary and sounds have been learned. If deafness comes at age six or later, a fairly good foundation in speech and language exists upon which a good teacher of the deaf can build passable speech with relative ease. At ages beyond eight or ten years, or more conservatively twelve, speech habits are well established, and the educational aim is one of maintenance and correction as far as speech is concerned.

Lipreading results, however, do not follow the same pattern as do those for speech in relation to age when deafness occurred. Results are much less predictable. Very often a person deafened in late youth or adulthood finds lipreading a very uncertain and difficult art, whereas a person born deaf may read the lips better than he can speak.

From the foregoing facts, it may be assumed that the number of persons using oral means of expressive communication would include a large proportion of those who had lost their hearing after the age of six years, and fewer of these would use oral means for reception (lipreading). This assumption is borne out by the data in Table 14.

All eighteen of those persons deafened after age twelve used speech for their expressive communication, but only eleven of the eighteen used lipreading. Of those who lost their hearing after age six, four-fifths used speech most frequently and only a little more than half used lipreading. Those who were deafened prior to age six were more consistent in the use of oral means of communication for expression and reception; 53 per cent used oral means for expression and 57 per cent for reception. Preferred means of communication were in similar proportions to those above, except that, of the respondents

---

*The word "taught" is used intentionally in this paragraph because understanding of communication of persons deafened early in life will not be complete unless it is remembered that their speech—all of it—has been patiently, laboriously *taught* to them.

TABLE 14
MEANS OF COMMUNICATION MOST FREQUENTLY USED
WITH HEARING PERSONS AT WORK, BY AGE
WHEN DEAFNESS OCCURRED

Age of Occurrence of Deafness	Means of Communication					
	Expressive			Receptive		
	Total	Oral	Non-Oral	Total	Oral	Non-Oral
Born deaf	26	15	11	26	14	12
Under 1 year	5	2	3	5	2	3
1 and under 3	12	6	6	12	8	4
3 and under 6	9	4	5	9	5	4
6 and under 12	16	9	7	16	7	9
12 and under 15	10	10		10	7	3
15 and over	8	8		8	4	4
Age unknown	1	1		1	1	
Total	87	55	32	87	48	39

whose deafness occurred before age six, only 39 per cent preferred oral means of reception.

The ratings of speech skills showed similar results in relation to age. As shown in Table 15, respondents whose deafness occurred after age six tended to rate their lipreading skill much lower than their skill in speech. The respondents deafened before age six rated themselves very much the same for both skills.

Of the thirty-six respondents rated highest in speech, twenty-three (64 per cent) were deafened after the age of six; on the other hand, only about one-third of the seventeen rated best in lipreading were deafened after age six. The respondents who were deafened early tended to rank lower on the scale but were more consistent as regards the two skills. Over two-thirds of those deafened after age six had almost perfectly understood speech, but the same could be said of the lipreading ability of only 18 per cent of them. Ratings by colleagues were higher for both groups on both skills but roughly similar to the pattern described above.

Comparison of individual ratings shows that, of the group whose deafness occurred before age six, thirty-three rated their lipreading skill the same as or better than their speech and eighteen rated their lipreading skill lower than their speech (assuming the rating scales are equal). Of those who had lost their hearing after age six, fourteen rated their lipreading skill the same as, or better than, their speech; twenty-one rated speech skill higher.

From the more or less uniform results with respect to age when

TABLE 15

SPEECH SKILLS, EXPRESSIVE AND RECEPTIVE, AS PERCEIVED
BY RESPONDENTS, BY AGE WHEN DEAFNESS OCCURRED

| Speech Skills | | Age When Deafness Occurred | | | |
| | | Under 6 Years | | Over 6 Years | |
	Total	Number	Per Cent	Number	Per Cent
Expressive:					
Associates understand:					
Practically all respondent says	36	13	25	23	68
Almost everything said	29	19	37	10	29
Occasional word or two	15	14	27	1	3
Respondent never speaks	3	3	6	—	—
No answer	3	3	6	—	—
Total	86*	52*	101	34	100
Receptive:					
Respondent understands:					
Almost everything said	17	11	21	6	18
Short conversation	37	18	35	19	56
Short, simple sentences	19	12	23	7	21
Occasional word or two	11	9	17	2	6
No answer	2	2	4	—	—
Total	86*	52*	100	34	101

*Omits one respondent whose age of occurrence of deafness is not known.

deafness occurred in relation to means of communication used and preferred by the respondents and their skills in speech and lipreading, the following conclusions seem reasonable: Persons deafened very early in life make less use of speech and find it less successful than do those deafened in late childhood or in the teens. However, those of the very early deafened who do learn to talk also achieve proficiency in lipreading more often than not. Persons who have lost their hearing after the age of six years generally retain good speech, which they use and prefer, but they do not attain so frequently the highest skill in lipreading and hence use it less frequently and prefer it even less.

A broad generalization from these facts would be that speech and lipreading are skills that not all deaf persons can acquire. Also, speech and lipreading are concomitant skills when they are learned; a person who has been *taught* speech generally has learned a reasonable skill in lipreading.

TRICKS AND DEVICES TO AID COMMUNICATION

From preceding pages of this chapter, it might seem that a deaf person's only communication problems are the mechanics of person-to-person conversation and that skill in speech and lipreading, however difficult to attain, would solve all of these. Such, of course, is not the case. Other problems do exist, ranging from tact in minimizing the impact of one's handicap on others to the more obvious problem of getting the most out of the telephone. There are many examples of ingenuity in getting around such barriers.

Perhaps the most easily understood of these problems is that of using the telephone. Another, a bit less obvious, is participation in a fast-moving conference where the speaker and the subject may change so rapidly that even the best lipreader is unable to follow. These two means of communication are extensively used in the working world and they can and do provide large barriers to a deaf man's progress. The approaches and results involved in meeting the two difficulties are discussed in detail in Chapter VI as on-the-job problems.

Other devices to aid communication are of more general application. One of these is to have a pad and pencil always ready when needed; thirty-seven respondents said that they do this. Some refined the technique: "Usually I print all my writing" and "I've learned to read upside down. Saves turning the paper around." Several, however, scorned this method, saying, "I never carry pad and pencil around," an attitude which seems to be connected with pride in lipreading ability and probably with early conditioning by parents and/or teachers to be "normal."

Another technique is to dominate the conversation, as:

> When I communicate with someone, I try to start the subject matter because if I know when they are talking about a certain subject, it is easier for me to follow. If they come along and start their own subject, well, I have to do a lot of groping around before I find out what they're talking about.
>
> Leading questions . . . I ask them questions which can be answered with a yes or no.

One respondent stresses clarity of expression: "I would say to have patience and put your ideas over clearly, use simple language. . . ."

A question asked if the respondent maneuvered his companion into the best light to help in lipreading. Many replied to the effect that they were not so obvious about it; their ideas and techniques are summed up in this reply:

> No, of course not. I am cagey. I case the joint ahead of time. I place myself with my back to the light. When I play cards and we change around and someone says, "Will you have this chair or that one?" I will say, "Oh, I'll take *that* one." I have a reason but I don't go around hanging up a sign advertising it.

Resignation to the incomplete understanding which often occurs when reading the lips was urged by one respondent:

> . . . I am talking about social chit chat. If you miss something, the world is not going to fall to pieces. . . . Some people just simply cannot be understood. Well, the impression is important. I will try to get them talking and will be interested even if I do not understand all they are saying. . . . Why, most people under those circumstances are perfectly happy, having a good time.

Devices to aid communication for the profoundly deaf boil down to ingenuity, foresight, patience and tact.

SUMMARY

On the whole, it may be said that speech and lipreading were of significant use to most of the respondents. At work, almost two-thirds of them used speech, and more than half used lipreading as their chief means of communication, supplementing these with writing as a second choice. Over 90 per cent of them used oral communication to some extent. This proportion was almost three times as great as that among the respondents in the *Survey of Occupational Conditions Among the Deaf* and half again as great as among nonteaching professionals in the *Survey*. Only a very few of the respondents in the study employed manual communication at work, although over 80 per cent of them used manual means with their deaf friends.

While the proportion using speech and lipreading at work was high, their preferences were less so, a little over half of them preferring to talk and less than half preferring lipreading as a mode of communication.

Confidence in expressive skills was high among the respondents, three-fourths of them stating that almost everything they said was understood by their co-workers. They had less faith in their lipreading

ability, only about one-fifth claiming to understand almost everything said to them. Colleagues rated the respondents higher; four-
fifths said that they understood almost everything the respondents
said to them and two-fifths that respondents understood almost everything said. High skill in speech was acquired without training by
most of the respondents; two-thirds of those with the best speech
had lost their hearing after the age of six years.

Practically none of the respondents were able to use hearing aids,
a result of the selection criteria, which required that reception be
chiefly visual. No other aids were mentioned except a pad and pencil and tact in social situations.

Chapter III

EDUCATION

BACKGROUND

The AUTOMATIC ASSUMPTION in approaching any group of professional workers is that they will be well educated. The assumption applies to deaf professional workers, but there is a complication. The importance of education to the deaf professional is colored by the difficulty of attaining that education. A child born deaf or deafened very early in life lacks the oral stimuli which form the basis for development of speech and, more importantly, language. The nature of learning language and developing speech makes the whole learning process laborious for this child. Substitutes must be developed—lipreading, observation, reading skill and every other avenue to the growing mind.

Everything that the severely deaf person learns must come to him through the eyes. The ever-present blare of radio and the conversation of adults around him are lost to the deaf child. With them is lost that extensive background of common knowledge and attitudes which every child with normal hearing accumulates unconsciously through daily contacts. Additionally, the deaf child's entire knowledge is structured and fed to him by another person; he is utterly dependent for the quality of his knowledge upon the quality of his teachers. He picks up none of the knowledge coming from conversations and communicative programs absorbed subconsciously by children who can hear.

In assessing educational difficulties of the child with early and severe deafness especial attention must be given to the difficulties of learning language. It is easy enough for the layman to realize that lack of hearing in the preschool years denies the deaf child all the assimilation from the earliest coos of its mother to the indirect conversation picked up from parents, siblings and playmates and the communication media. More difficult to comprehend, however, is the confusion of grammatical syntax which arises from the skip-and-guess technique of lipreading and from the ideographic nature of the sign language. Fortunate is the deaf person who has early realized the joys of reading and has thus been exposed to language well expressed. Since language is the tool for both acquisition and expression of knowledge, the impact of the deaf person's difficulties with language cannot be exaggerated. The problems are especially severe as regards the professions in which communication is of integral importance.

The preceding description then, represents a deaf candidate for the professions. If he was deafened early, his preschool days have been handicapped by vocabulary gaps, lack of general association with other children and possibly psychic trauma from his isolated position. Once in school, his learning has been limited more or less to the knowledge which his teacher could give him and the manner by which she gave it and even that knowledge has been, in many cases, only dimly perceived because of communication difficulties.

The strongly stimulated and well-retained learning from play activities and spontaneous inquiry is infrequently expressed for the deaf child in English. Even the schoolroom learning of traditional subject matter is limited by the time taken up by speech and lipreading, rhythm training and the vocational arts, however useful these specialized fields may be. Finally, there is tremendous variation in the quality of the education offered in the various schools for the deaf throughout the nation. Hence, it may be said that achieving even the plateau of higher education is a remarkable accomplishment in the path to the formidable peak represented by these respondents' accomplishments.

AGE OF OCCURRENCE OF DEAFNESS

In assessing a deaf child's potential for learning, educators are very much concerned with the age at which deafness occurred. Since the age of occurrence has a strong effect upon language acquisition and hence upon the whole gamut of education, an offhand hypothesis from this professional attitude would be that very few of those persons who became deaf prior to age three (first year of preschool training) or age six (first year of regular school) would be able to acquire competence in professional fields, where communication is of such vital importance.

For the group of respondents in this study such an extreme conclusion does not hold. Table 16 shows that for 49 per cent of the respondents, deafness occurred before the age of three years; 30 per cent were born deaf. The proportion of the respondents in this study who were born deaf compares closely with the proportion of such among the 10,101 respondents in the Bigman-Lunde[2] study (28.5. per cent), as is shown in Table 16. Deafness occurred prior to age six, a critical year as regards education, for 60 per cent of the present respondents as compared to 74.4 per cent of all respondents in the *Survey of Occupational Conditions Among the Deaf.* In other words, the proportions as to age of occurrence of deafness are fairly similar for the general population of deaf people and for those in professional occupations as represented by the respondents in this study.

TABLE 16
AGE WHEN DEAFNESS OCCURRED*

Age When Deafness Occurred	Respondents Number	Per Cent	Respondents in The Survey of Occupational Conditions Among the Deaf Per Cent
Born deaf	26	30	28.5
Under 1	5	6	7.9
1 and under 3	12	14	38.0
3 and under 6	9	10	
6 and under 12	16	18	
12 and under 15	10	11	12.4
15 and over	8	9	
Age unknown	1	1	4.9
Not reported			8.3
Total	87	99	100.0 (10,101)

*Respondents and total respondents reported in *The Survey of Occupational Conditions Among the Deaf.*

The findings presented in Table 16 are of great and encouraging importance to educators of the deaf. They indicate a high potential existing among early deafened people, a group with many educational handicaps. This potential is a challenge to defeatist attitudes. Perhaps it also points to an examination of curricula, methods and philosophy in the education of these people.

SCHOOLS
Types of Schools for the Deaf

In any examination of the education of deaf persons, the manner of their early education must receive careful consideration. There is a considerable variety of school situations open to the young deaf child. The variations occur in the administrative setup of the schools and in the basic philosophy underlying their approach to communication in the educational process.

The *American Annals of the Deaf,* the professional journal of educators of the deaf, divides schools for the deaf into five administrative classifications: Public (state-supported) residential schools, private and denominational residential schools, public day schools (separate schools for deaf pupils within the public school system), public day classes (a unit for deaf pupils within a single public school) and private and denominational day classes.[1] The chief administrative differences among these schools may be outlined as follows: Residential schools have larger populations, allowing more homogeneous class assignments but keep pupils away from home for long periods. Day schools allow the child to be home daily and place him in proximity with normal children. Day classes operate as day schools but have the defects of the one-room schoolhouse, i.e., a single teacher coping with various grade levels.

Two divergences in educational approach characterizes the schools: oral communication and integration with children who hear. The differences are a matter of extent; almost all schools teach speech and lipreading and all deaf children have some degree of contact with normal children. At one extreme on the scale of attitudes about communication is a school environment which aims for the use of speech and lipreading in all situations and sends deaf children into public school classes of hearing children at high school level or sometimes at the elementary level. At the other extreme, the school provides a primary department where manual spelling supplements the oral approach and intermediate and advanced departments where both oral communication and manual signs and spelling are used; schools at this end of the continuum rarely provide for integration into the public schools. As a generalization, it might be said that most public residential schools tend to adopt a combination of communication methods while most private and day schools for the deaf incline toward the strictly oral method.

Since there is a variety in degree of adherence to these principles, the effects of school policies upon graduates of the schools for the deaf vary. One extreme result is the shunning of deaf companions and unrealistically hopeful attitudes about participating with people who hear; the other extreme is the minimizing of contact with hearing persons almost to the point of isolation from the general public, that is, socializing almost entirely among deaf people. The usual attitude of deaf persons is somewhere between the two poles. Squabbling of educators over these extremes has been a baneful influence on educational progress.

Types of Schools Ever Attended

The regular public schools and the residential schools for the deaf predominated in the education of the respondents; over three-fourths of them had been, at one time or another, in a residential school for the deaf or a school for the general public, according to Table 17. Among the deaf people covered by the *Survey of Occupational Conditions Among the Deaf,* the predominance among schools ever attended was almost wholly (90.8 per cent) with the "state residential school."*

The dominance of the state residential school among the respondents of the Bigman-Lunde survey is further emphasized by the fact that 68.4 per cent of the respondents received *all* of their education at these schools. Such is not the case for the present respondents; only twenty-three of the eighty-seven had spent all their precollege years in one type of school. Of those twenty-three, fifteen had attended public residential schools for the deaf; two, private residential schools for the deaf; one, day classes for the deaf; six, regular public schools.

---

*These data are probably biased by the method of selection used in the study. Interviews were conducted by representatives of the National Association of the Deaf, generally at gatherings sponsored by state or local organizations of the deaf. Because of this method, the respondents were, by and large, products of the state schools for the deaf. *The American Annals of the Deaf* in the January 1958 (statistical) number, shows pupils of state residential schools for the deaf as comprising 60.0 per cent of the total pupil population reported.

TABLE 17
TYPE OF SCHOOL EVER ATTENDED*

Type of School	Respondents		Respondents in The Survey of Occupational Conditions Among the Deaf[a]
	Number	Per Cent	Per Cent
Schools for the deaf: Residential:			
Public[t]	48	55	
Private	19	22	
Total	67	77	90.8[‡]
Day:			
Schools[§]	20	23	
Classes‖	9	10	
Total	29	33	12.7[¶]
Schools for the general population:			
Public	54	62	
Private	14	16	
Total	68	78	15.7**
Others (tutors)	7	8	
Total respondents	87[tt]	—[tt]	—[tt]

*Respondents and Respondents in *The Survey of Occupational Conditions Among the Deaf.*
†Includes Preparatory Department, Gallaudet College.
‡"State residential school."
§Occupies a building for exclusive use of deaf and hard of hearing pupils.
‖Shares occupancy of a building with pupils of normal hearing.
¶"Day school."
**"Hearing school."
††Columns add to more than 87 and 100 per cent because of multiple answers.

Types of Schools Attended the Longest

More pertinent, perhaps, than the type of school ever attended is the type of school attended the longest, on the assumption that the longer attendance would result in a greater influence upon the person attending. Table 18 shows what types of school the respondents attended the longest.

Fifty-six, or almost two-thirds of the respondents received most of their elementary and secondary education in schools for the deaf, more than half of these (thirty) at public residential schools for the deaf. Of the thirty-one who attended schools for hearing children, most had gone to regular public schools.

As might be expected, the respondents who had attended schools

TABLE 18

TYPE OF ELEMENTARY AND SECONDARY SCHOOL
ATTENDED THE LONGEST

Type of School	Number	Per Cent
Schools for the deaf:	(56)	(64)
Residential:		
Public	30	34
Private	10	11
Day:		
School	11	13
Class	4	5
Other	1*	1
Schools for the hearing:	(31)	(36)
Public	26	30
Private	4	5
Other	1†	1
Total	87	100

*Five years each in a private residential and a day school
for the deaf.
†Six years each in private and public schools for hearing
persons.

for hearing children the longest were largely those whose hearing loss
had occurred relatively late in childhood. Table 19 reveals that 74
per cent of those who had attended public schools the longest had
lost their hearing after age six, whereas the proportion whose deafness had occurred before the age of six was about 87 per cent for
those educated in public residential schools for the deaf and 74 per
cent of the respondents educated in other schools for the deaf.

TABLE 19

AGE OF OCCURRENCE OF DEAFNESS
BY TYPE OF SCHOOL ATTENDED LONGEST

Age of Occurrence of Deafness	Total	Schools for the Deaf				Schools for the Hearing	
		Public Residential		Others			
		Number	Per Cent	Number	Per Cent	Number	Per Cent
Born deaf	26	12	40	9	35	5	16
Under 6	26	14	47	10	38	2	6
6 and under 12	16	2	7	6	23	8	26
12 and over	18	2	7	1	4	15	48
Age unknown	1	—	—	—	—	1	3
Total	87	30	101	26	100	31	99

YEARS SPENT IN ELEMENTARY AND SECONDARY SCHOOLS

In considering the total years spent in schools at the elementary and secondary levels, certain peculiarities must be recognized. As has been stated, the deaf child lacks the informal educative stimuli which come through the ear to hearing preschool children. More time must be spent with the deaf child in formal schooling to make up for this lack. Instruction in the difficult arts of speech and lip-reading further complicates and extends the educational program. Vocational training also takes a sizable part of the educational day. To accomplish these extra tasks, many schools for the deaf extend the educational period by attaching one to four preschool years and by allowing pupils to remain in school until age twenty-one if necessary. It is reasonable, then, to expect that the deaf person's precollege education will be longer than that of by his hearing peers. Table 20 shows the number of years of the respondents' elementary and secondary schooling.

TABLE 20

YEARS SPENT IN ELEMENTARY AND SECONDARY SCHOOLS

Years	Number	Per Cent
1-8	2	2
9-11	15	17
12	24	28
13	18	21
14	11	13
15	15	17
16	1	1
18	1	1
Total	87	100

Perhaps the greatest significance in the table is the high percentage (53 per cent) of deaf persons who had spent more than the usual twelve years in elementary and secondary schools. The long stay in the elementary and secondary schools by deaf persons is further emphasized by the fact that few, if any, of them had completed, in the school for the deaf, a full high school education comparable to that in the public high schools. To continue on to college and possibly through graduate study, as most of the respondents had, represents a very considerable investment of time in preparation for a career. If one adds the college years, the total time spent by a deaf person in acquiring an education is sixteen to twenty-two years for the bachelor's degree. This means graduation at twenty-two to twenty-eight years of age. If the deaf person goes on to the master's and doctor's degrees and then undergoes the usual starvation period typical for a professional person, virtually half his life is gone before he can be said to be established in his career.

Table 21 indicates that over 60 per cent of the respondents who were deafened before age six spent more than the usual twelve years in the elementary and secondary grades, whereas only 41 per cent of those deafened after age six had spent more than twelve years in these grades. That a greater number of those respondents deafened early in life had spent a longer time in school can be attributed both to the handicap of deafness and to the structure of their educational environment, e.g., school time given to special training.

TABLE 21

AGE OF OCCURRENCE OF DEAFNESS, BY YEARS
SPENT IN ELEMENTARY AND SECONDARY SCHOOLS

Age of Occurrence of Deafness	Total	Under 13 Years	13 Years and Over
Under 6 years	53	21	32
6 years and over	34	20	14
Total	87	41	46

The respondents with the longer terms in elementary and secondary schools tended to come chiefly from the schools for the deaf. Of the forty-six who were in these grades for thirteen years or more, thirty-six (78 per cent) attended schools for the deaf the longest; of the forty-one whose elementary and secondary schooling required twelve years or less, only twenty, or less than half, had attended chiefly schools for the deaf (Table 22).

Completion of precollege education in less than thirteen years was accomplished by 68 per cent of those respondents who had attended nonspecialized schools the longest but by only 36 per cent of respondents who had attended schools for the deaf. Within the schools for the deaf, 43 per cent of respondents attending public residential schools took less than thirteen years, whereas 28 per cent of those in private and day schools or day classes finished in less than thirteen years.

TABLE 22

YEARS SPENT IN ELEMENTARY AND SECONDARY SCHOOLS,
BY TYPE OF SCHOOL ATTENDED LONGEST

| Type of School Attended Longest | *Years Spent in Elementary and Secondary Schools* | | |
	Total	*Under 13 Years*	*13 Years and Over*
Schools for the deaf:	(56)	(20)	(36)
Residential:			
Public	30	13	17
Private	10	3	7
Day:			
School	11	3	8
Class	4	1	3
Other	1		1*
Schools for the general population:	(31)	(21)	(10)
Public	26	18	8
Private:			
Residential	1		1
Day	3	2	1
Other	1	1†	
Total	87	41	46

*Five years in private residential and five years in day schools, plus four years in public schools for hearing persons.

†Six years in public schools and six years in private day schools.

HIGHEST EDUCATIONAL LEVEL ATTAINED

To what extent did the respondents prepare themselves educationally for their professions? Is it necessary for deaf persons to train extensively—possibly more extensively than do people who hear? Table 23 shows the highest educational level attained by the respondents.

Age when deafness occurred seems, from Table 24, to bear upon the extent of academic success. A larger proportion (35 per cent)

TABLE 23

HIGHEST EDUCATIONAL LEVEL ATTAINED
BY RESPONDENTS

| *Educational Level Completed* | *Respondents* | |
	Number	*Per Cent*
Twelfth grade	5	6
Some college	21	24
Bachelor's degree	22	25
Some graduate study	17	20
Master's degree	13	15
Post-master's study	4	5
Doctor's degree	5	6
Total	87	101

of those deafened after age six than those (19 per cent) deafened before age six received the master's degree or better; 51 per cent of the early deafened as against 35 per cent of those deafened after age six received the bachelor's degree.

TABLE 24

HIGHEST EDUCATIONAL LEVEL ATTAINED,
BY AGE WHEN DEAFNESS OCCURRED

Highest Educational Level Attained	Total	Age When Deafness Occurred			
		Before Age 6		Age 6 and Over	
		Number	Per Cent	Number	Per Cent
Grade 12	5	4	8	1	3
Some college	21	12	23	9	26
Bachelor's degree Some graduate work	39	27	51	12	35
Master's degree	17	7	13	10	29
Doctor's degree	5	3	6	2	6
Total	87	53	101	34	99

Respondents who had attended chiefly Gallaudet College as undergraduates more frequently earned the bachelor's degree but did not tend to press on to the graduate degrees as frequently as those who spent most of their undergraduate years in a college for the general public, according to Table 25.

Of the Gallaudet students, 91 per cent received bachelor's degrees as compared to 63 per cent of the non-Gallaudet respondents. However, 29 per cent of the non-Gallaudet respondents had earned the master's degree or better and five of these had doctorates, whereas

TABLE 25

HIGHEST EDUCATIONAL LEVEL ATTAINED,
BY COLLEGE ATTENDED DURING
UNDERGRADUATE YEARS

Highest Educational Level Attained	Total	College Attended as an Undergraduate					
		Gallaudet Only	Most Years at Gallaudet	Most Years at Another College	Another College Only	Other	No College
Grade 12	5						5
Some college	21	3		1	16	1*	
Bachelor's degree Graduate study	39	17	6	1	15		
Master's degree	17	6	2		9		
Doctor's degree	5				5		
Total	87	26	8	2	45	1	5

*Attended graduate school only.

only 23 per cent of Gallaudet respondents had master's degrees and none had earned the doctor's degree. Probably one causative factor was Gallaudet College's unaccredited status during the years when many respondents were students there and the consequent difficulty in matriculating at graduate schools. In addition, the large universities have a variety of graduate programs to offer the students; Gallaudet's graduate work is limited to the education of the deaf. Another possible factor might have been the economic level of most of Gallaudet students; not many of them could have afforded more than part-time graduate study.

It is also probable that less drive is needed to enter and graduate from Gallaudet College than is required of a deaf person to do the same at a college for those who hear, with all the limitations and difficulties implicit in such a situation. It is reasonable to expect more momentum among those deaf persons who matriculated as undergraduates at regular colleges.

Another factor related to academic achievement seems to be the type of school at which the respondents received most of their elementary and secondary education. Table 26 shows that only 15 per cent of respondents who had attended mainly schools for the deaf had received graduate degrees, whereas 44 per cent of those who had attended nonspecialized schools had received the higher degrees.

There seems to have been some relationship between the occupational fields in which respondents were employed and the extent of their education, as shown in Table 27. Most respondents employed in art and architecture lacked college degrees. Almost half of the

TABLE 26

HIGHEST EDUCATIONAL LEVEL ATTAINED, BY TYPE OF
ELEMENTARY AND SECONDARY SCHOOL ATTENDED LONGEST

Highest Educational Level Attained	Total	Type of School Attended Longest			
		Schools for the Deaf		Public Schools	
		Number	Per Cent	Number	Per Cent
Grade 12	5	5	9		
Some college	21	13	24	8	25
Bachelor's degree	39	29	53	10	31
Master's degree	17	7	13	10	31
Doctor's degree	5	1	2	4	13
Total	87	55	101	32	100

TABLE 27

OCCUPATIONAL CLASSIFICATION, BY
HIGHEST EDUCATIONAL LEVEL ATTAINED

Occupational Classification	Total	Grade 12	Highest Educational Level Attained				
			Some College	Bachelor's Degree	Some Graduate Study	Master's Degree	Doctor's Degree
Art and architecture	8	1	6	1			
Business	5		1	2	1	1	
Chemistry	23		2	5	5	9	2
Engineering	25	2	10	7	4	2	
Library work and museum work	5	1	1	2		1	
Mathematics and statistics	9			3	5	1	
Other scientists	7	1		1	1	2	2
Miscellaneous	5		1	1	1	1	1
Total	87	5	21	22	17	17	5

engineers also lacked degrees; of the twelve out of twenty-five in engineering and the seven out of eight in art and architecture without degrees, four in each group were draftsmen and two were designers, occupations in which the level of educational accomplishment varies greatly. Of the respondents in the sciences as a group (chemistry, engineering, mathematics, statistics and other sciences), 77 per cent had college degrees, whereas only 52 per cent of the respondents in all other occupations possessed degrees. More than half of the scientists, but only about one in four of the other respondents, had done some graduate study.

The respondents studied at ninety-eight different colleges and universities, which are listed in Appendix B. Table 28 shows the types of colleges and universities attended by the respondents and the types of degrees earned.

TABLE 28

TYPES OF COLLEGES AND UNIVERSITIES ATTENDED
AND DEGREES EARNED BY RESPONDENTS

Type of College or University	Number of Institutions	Degrees Earned			
		Bachelor	Master	Doctor	None
State university or college	27	8	8	3	22
Private university	20	5	12	1	11
Private college	17	7			23
Gallaudet College	1	34			2
City college	10	4	2		11
Technical institutions	16	6	1		14
Law school	3	1		1	1
Junior college	4				4
Total	98	65*	23*	5	88

*Some respondents earned two degrees at one level.

No pattern is evident in the choice of institutions for undergraduate study except that an expected large number of respondents received their bachelor's degrees from Gallaudet College. Gallaudet did not, at the time of the respondents' attendance, confer graduate degrees upon deaf persons. The master's and doctor's degrees held by respondents came largely from the bigger colleges and universities.

Does occupational status of the father influence the extent of educational achievement among deaf persons as it has been shown to do among the general population? Table 29 indicates that such may have been the case with eighty-four of the respondents. The proportion of respondents whose fathers were white-collar workers increased as the level of educational achievement rose. Of the fifty-four fathers who were white-collar workers, fifty were in professional or managerial positions.

TABLE 29

HIGHEST EDUCATIONAL LEVEL ATTAINED,
BY OCCUPATION OF RESPONDENT'S FATHER

| | | | Occupation of the Father | | | |
| Highest Educational Level Attained | Total | | White-Collar Workers | | Blue-Collar and Service Workers | |
	Number	Per Cent	Number	Per Cent	Number	Per Cent
Less than bachelor's degree	25	100	13	52	12	48
Bachelor's degree	38	100	23	61	15	39
Master's and doctor's degrees	21	100	18*	86	3	14
Total†	84	100	54	64	30	36

*All 5 respondents with doctorates are from white-collar families.
†Excludes 2 whose fathers were dead during the respondent's school days and 1 from whom no answer was received.

Insofar as income measures "success," Table 30 seems to indicate that higher education pays off for deaf professional people. The median income of the respondents was $7,615, which compares well with the $7,036 median income of salaried professional workers in the 1960 general population,[15] remembering, however, that the respondent group excludes teachers and ministers, who would probably have pulled the median figure down. As the succeeding levels of educational attainment were reached there was a higher percentage of respondents who earned above the median class interval ($6,000-7,999). Of those below the bachelor's degree, 35 per cent earned $8,000 or over; of those with bachelor's degrees, 39 per cent; of those with master's or doctor's degrees, 64 per cent.

Fields of Study

Of the forty-seven respondents who attended regular colleges or universities a majority (twenty-eight) majored in the natural sciences. Economics and business administration were taken by six and English by three respondents; one each took degrees in mechanical arts, architecture, agriculture and the liberal arts. One respondent did graduate work in library science but had no bachelor's degree. The thirty-

TABLE 30

HIGHEST EDUCATIONAL LEVEL ATTAINED,
BY INCOME LEVEL

Educational Level Completed	Total	$4,000-$5,999	$6,000-$7,999	$8,000-$9,999	$10,000-$11,999	$12,000 or Over
Grade 12	5			1		
Some college	21	2	2	7		1
Bachelor's degree	22	6	7	2	1	2
Some graduate study	17	11	6	7	1	2
Master's degree	17	2	5	7	1	
Doctor's degree	5	2	1	3	1	
Total	87	23	26	27	4	7

four who attended Gallaudet College received degrees in the arts and sciences. Although the college during those years did offer fairly extensive curricula in chemistry, library science and home economics, no majors were available to the students.

DIFFICULTIES AT COLLEGE DUE TO DEAFNESS

The bright college years may not be so bright for a deaf person. In fact, he may find them quite difficult. Difficulties often start before the deaf person matriculates; they take the form of doubts and prejudices as to his abilities. Once registered, he may find lectures incomprehensible, seminars impossible and the intricacies of academic requirements tremendously complicated by his handicap (foreign languages, for example).

The situation being what it is, it may be considered remarkable that only seventeen of the sixty-six respondents considered the difficulties they encountered to be great. Table 31 shows the various

TABLE 31

DEGREES OF DIFFICULTY* AT COLLEGE DUE TO DEAFNESS: RESPONDENTS EVER ATTENDING COLLEGES OR UNIVERSITIES FOR PERSONS WHO HEAR

Degree of Difficulty	Total Respondents	Gallaudet Students Graduate Years Only	Other Undergraduate Students		
			Total	Undergraduate Years	Graduate Years
No difficulties	8	2	6	3	3
Negligible	21	3	18	10	8
Moderate	18	4	14	10	4
Great	15	8	7	5	2
Caused to abandon studies	2	1	1	1	
Other difficulties than deafness	1		1	1	
Other	1†		1		1
Total‡	66	18	48	30	18

*Interpretation of degrees of difficulty: *Negligible:* "not much trouble," "it was easy"; respondents minimized difficulties. *Moderate:* Respondents mentioned difficulties but used *no* qualifying words or phrases such as "not much" or "a great deal." *Great:* "very boring," "lots of trouble" or any use of superlatives to describe difficulties.

†Completed college education before becoming deaf.

‡The table omits 16 respondents who received the bachelor's degree from Gallaudet College but took no graduate work and 5 who did not go to college; two of those who went to Gallaudet had previously attended other colleges and reported great difficulties due to deafness.

degrees of difficulty perceived by those who had attended regular colleges or universities.

Over two-fifths of the respondents classified their difficulties as none or negligible and more than two-thirds said the difficulties had been moderate or less. This minimizing of difficulties may have resulted from the dimming of memories by time, the aggressiveness of the respondents, their modesty or any number of conditioning reasons. The fact remains, however, that all did recognize the existence of difficulties or limitations. Those who considered them negligible nevertheless cited accommodation by their friends, the professors and others:

> My friends were very considerate about telling me about announcements . . . and they were very helpful with lecture work. . . .
>
> I had no difficulties . . . all my teachers had a lot of patience with me.
>
> Nothing much . . . I had myself excused from all lectures. . . . Most of them accepted that. Some refused, so I had to change my program to whoever would accept me. (Respondent was not seeking a degree.)

Others took a dimmer view:

> When I look back, I must admit to myself that I'm surprised I went through. Of course I missed a lot of material from the lectures. I had to depend a lot on the boys sitting alongside of me. I had to make up for that by doing a lot of studying at home. I did not participate very much in extra-curricular activities simply because I had to devote so much time to studying at home.
>
> I felt that if I could hear, I would definitely have done better work; however, whatever difficulties I experienced were compensated by awareness of my shortcomings and to know where my limitations would be and not to go up a blind alley.

At the graduate level, difficulties seemed to be less:

> Requirements . . . at the graduate level were tailored to specific needs . . . so I found graduate work very much easier and pleasanter and more satisfying than undergraduate work.
>
> I found the professors much more cooperative in my graduate school studies.

The situation was not entirely one of struggling against odds. One student was given copies of the professor's notes and found, at term's end, that all his classmates wanted to use them. Another said, "Many times I did not have to have help and I helped other people." Another:

> I didn't make any large effort to understand the professors, but I learned enough to get a practically straight A average by studying books and taking notes from fellow students.

Deafness caused some difficulties that provided amusement in retrospect.

> I sat up all one night studying for the driest course on record . . . and I went to take the examination and no one showed up except me. I found out that in the first week of the course the professor had announced there would be no written examination. . . . I was primed to the gills with no place to unload it.

The Gallaudet College graduates who had gone on to regular colleges and universities rated their difficulties in reverse proportions to the general trend. The attitude is understandable, since there was little or no problem of communication during their undergraduate years in contrast to the difficulties met when they attended regular colleges and universities as graduate students.

Questions were asked regarding three of the chief problems of course work for a deaf person at college: lecture notes, consultation with the professor and discussions in classes and seminars. The respondents were asked how they managed these problems.

Of the sixty-six respondents who attended colleges and universities for hearing persons, fifty said that they had depended on classmates for their notes; twenty-three did extensive outside reading to supplement what they had acquired from lectures; five sought front seats for lipreading. The total of these methods exceeds the number of respondents, since some cited more than one method. Selecting the person from whom to copy notes was the chief point of technique. Several of the respondents asked two or three students to make carbon copies of their notes, thus having possibly the best notes in class. Some would watch for:

> . . . a very busy person taking notes and the next day I would walk right over to that person and explain my problem and get a seat next to him or her. . . .

Another:

> I mostly sat beside the girls as they have more notes than the men do.

Subject matter of the course affects the note-taking problem, too:

> One of the advantages of taking science courses lies in the fact that there's a great deal of board discussion and visual education aids. With the aid of notes from one of the students and the visual education aids and the regular study assignments, I do not believe that I was at any disadvantage over the other students.

> English was tough. . . . All the teachers were talking all day through. I didn't understand what was going on. . . . I took mathematics, science and physics; they always write problems on the board.

It is significant that only five depended on a front seat for lipreading. The variables of lighting, speech habits of the professors, the respondent's position and so on make lipreading a doubtful vehicle for classroom communication, however competent a lip-reader may be in person-to-person conversation.

Managing communication with the professors divided into two technical aspects: when and how. Of the sixty-six respondents attending regular colleges and universities, forty-nine did seek help from the professors, thirty-five by seeking him after class and twenty-one by asking questions in class. Some used both methods. Some respondents hesitated to ask questions in class, fearing the lag between the spoken word and their questions:

> Very often the notes lagged behind the discussion so that if I wanted to speak up—even if I did and I wasn't a particularly bashful person— what I had to say would have been too late. So I didn't say it.

One respondent said, "I always felt that I would take away time that might be given to other students if I asked questions during class." The problems of speech clarity, tonal quality appropriate to the setting and possible interruption stymied some; one respondent said:

> I very rarely asked a question in class time. When I did, I had one of the people sitting next to me ask the question for me. (This respondent had good person-to-person speech, which he used extensively.)

Another problem of relations with professors was the professor's reaction to the discovery that one of his students was deaf. Many of the respondents made a practice of visiting their professors before classes began to explain their situation and their needs. Respondents' views of their professors' attitudes varied:

In most cases I found the professors not very helpful. . . . In one case, one professor did not want me in his class. . . . I was not allowed to take that course.

Perhaps two or three of my college instructors showed some evidence of irritation in the early phases of getting acquainted with the fact that they had a deaf student in class. These people were very few and far between. The average instructor was not only glad to see me but very cooperative.

Seminars and class discussions proved one of the most difficult problems. In twenty-two cases respondents did not attend such classes; twelve were excused, and for ten no seminars were required. Of those who did attend, nineteen took no part in the discussions; six depended on a fellow student to relay the gist of the discussion; four merely presented their topic and answered questions. Two cut the seminar classes, one receiving a low grade and the other failing that course. Many indicated this to have been a major problem, as:

That's my biggest problem. . . . I can understand one or two people all right, but I can't understand a group.

I had a hard time because in most classes the professors assigned me a front row seat so I could see him closer and, as a result, if a student in back of me asked a question, by the time I turned around the question would already have been answered.

No true remedy had been worked out for this problem, but a number of palliatives had been devised by respondents:

I found it best to obtain advance information as to what the seminar would be about . . . If I had an agenda, I would have no problem understanding the discussion. Otherwise, I was lost.

There were some instructors who would pass a note to me when they wanted me to enter the discussion.

The procedure was not much different from an ordinary class. The people who sat next to me again took notes. It was difficult to follow what was going on very well. I got the major points anyway. If I had a paper to give myself, I would have one of my classmates read it. I would answer any questions that the members of the seminar raised. They would have to write these questions to me.

I usually identified myself with one other person who could understand me and whom I could understand and we would participate in such classes as one person, usually after a period of time.

Two respondents did not participate for reasons expressed thus:

> It's my feeling that class discussions are of very little value. You have a group of immature people discussing a subject that they don't know much about. Each of them is trying to impress the others with how much he knows, how smart he is, how clever he is or the novelty of his thoughts. I think class discussions are greatly overrated.

A respondent made the following suggestion:

> It might be that other students trying to take part in seminars and open discussion could benefit by establishing procedure with the instructor or discussion leader. In that procedure, a deaf person might very well ask for the privilege of being first to open discussion on a new topic; then his ideas would be fresh and those who have had an opportunity to hear all the discussion would be able to add to it.

Almost three-fourths of the respondents who went to colleges and universities for the general public said that there were no academic requirements which they were unable to meet because of their deafness. The most frequent unmet subject matter requirements were speech classes (nine) and foreign languages (four). Group discussions were the leading technical difficulties (oral examinations, three; seminars, two). One respondent said, "I wasn't able to take part in the laboratory work; the machines were dangerous."

A large number (forty-seven) of the sixty-six respondents who went to regular colleges did not report any other problems; thirty-seven of these specifically stated that they had no problems other than those of the classroom just discussed and ten did not reply to this question. Twelve respondents mentioned social problems, such as missing out on the bull sessions, not attending social affairs, feeling out of place. Only one of these twelve was from Gallaudet College and, of the eighteen Gallaudet people, he was the only one who reported problems of that sort. Of course, this situation does not indicate that Gallaudet College has some magic formula to dissolve all social barriers of deafness. The Gallaudet graduates were all at the graduate level, where the social aspect of college life is of little importance, and they were much more adult and more experienced than undergraduates generally are.

Two extremes of adjustment to college social life are expressed below:

> I felt out of place. I was the only person in —— who was deaf. And

as far as social life was concerned, I couldn't participate. I was able to read lips pretty well and I was able to have a couple of friends whom I was able to talk to once in a while, but, aside from that, there was nothing I could do about social life in college.

I went to many, many social events, almost every week end. . . . I joined in the intramurals; I participated in the technical society.

The middle course was described by one respondent thus:

I had enough extra curricular activities to keep me busy and I was quite happy throughout my college work, but I could not feel at ease at most of the social functions.

The same respondent reported:

I had some strain when trying to take part in any extended effort in oral presentation or classroom discussions. I had no difficulties with oral reporting (he had lost his hearing at age fifteen), but if I had to give a seminar report of half-hour or forty-five-minute duration, I was exhausted at the end of the job and so tense I would be tired for a day or so afterward.

Two respondents made this recommendation:

I wouldn't recommend that a deaf person go to a city college. A small college out of town. He has a much better social life. The boys and girls are much nicer to him.

The eighty-two respondents who went to college were asked what changes, if any, they would make if they had their undergraduate years to live over. Probes were made about choice of college and major field of study. Of the thirty-four respondents who had attended Gallaudet College, nine would have changed to another college, seven of them because of instructional or curricular inadequacies. Of the forty-eight who had attended other colleges than Gallaudet, twenty-two would have changed, eight because of communication problems (four to Gallaudet and four to another, smaller, college), six because of instructional or curricular inadequacies and two because of the distance from home.

Opinions as to the value of attending Gallaudet College showed considerable divergence. Its proponents took the view that the undergraduate years are formative and that character development and the social aspects of undergraduate life outweigh the curricular and instructional aspects. Rapport with one's peers, they felt, would be better accomplished at Gallaudet, where communication is no problem, and hence a fuller participation in student affairs and classroom activities would be more likely there. (At the time most of the respondents were at Gallaudet, the college was very small and not accredited.) This view was expressed by one respondent thus:

> I think Gallaudet . . . fills a tremendous need. The undergraduate is a leavening person. The (deaf) person has an opportunity to function as a full person or as a member of a group; if he's in a college for the hearing, he's just a fringe person . . . never a part of the real stream of college life.

The opposite case was stated by another respondent:

> I think that education of the deaf should be improved, breaking out of the . . . Gallaudet-deaf school circle. They are very proud of Gallaudet, but they don't see the limitations it has imposed on them . . . those who have acquired the ability to use oral conversation and to understand oral conversation have the best jobs in most cases. There are a few totally deaf people I know who have done some good things professionally but very few. . . . It seems to be the attitude of the deaf schools that doesn't inspire them to do better than they do. . . . I think it's the teachers who teach them when they are small who can give them a view of something bigger than the vocational arts . . . children go up to these schools and then they go back (as teachers) and they have formed a little world of their own. And it's like going around in an orbit in there and it's hopeless.

Another took a curricular view:

> A good liberal arts background is an excellent basis upon which to build a professional background. Consequently, my advice to all seriously deaf persons is to go to Gallaudet first, then specialize elsewhere in schools better equipped to give first rate technical training.

Some who had been only to colleges for hearing persons recognized a lack in their undergraduate lives:

> If I had my undergraduate years to live over, I would try to be more of an extrovert. . . . I did not volunteer for anything. . . . I would try to sell myself better, to put myself across better than I did as a college student.
>
> I think I would have benefited greatly if I had had an opportunity to make better adjustments to social problems before I entered college. It may be that some special training might be made available to prospective students entering high school or college.

The remedy for the problem of being a fringe person was, for some, to go to a small college:

> I very much favor a small college for the first two years and then after adjustment to social life and after carrying the college work far enough to have a pretty good idea of where you want to go in the way of specializing for a career, then go to a larger school which is better equipped for that specialty.

Only seventeen would have changed their major field of study during their undergraduate years: eleven would have changed to the field in which they were employed, six to a different field.

The respondents were asked about education received elsewhere than in college classrooms. Fifty-seven said they did undertake some sort of additional educational effort. Thirty-one of them had taken correspondence courses, eleven had gone to vocational schools, sixteen had had formal on-the-job training. Two had been in business college and one had been tutored. For about half of those who did take extra training, it lasted for less than a year; eleven were at it for three years or more. Thirty-nine said they studied voluntarily and ten at the suggestion or request of their employers (for seven of these ten, the training was on-the-job). The remainder did not reply.

Fifty respondents assigned value to this training, four denied value and three did not reply. Values mentioned were chiefly increased skill or self-confidence. Fewer than half of the respondents saw advancement or increase in compensation as a direct result of their extra study.

CONCLUSIONS

The major conclusion about professional education for deaf people is that they are educable to the highest degree, although the process may take, on the average, a year or so longer than for other persons. People familiar with deaf adults recognized this fact long ago. However, for the uninitiated, it is worth repeating that these respondents include five who had earned the doctor's degree; seventeen, the master's; thirty-nine, the bachelor's and twenty-one, some sort of college training.

Most of those earning higher degrees had been educated in the regular public schools and had had fathers in white-collar jobs.

Most of the respondents reported encountering little difficulty at college due to their deafness, although most of them were aware that difficulties existed. These difficulties arose from the respondents' efforts to secure lecture notes, to communicate with professors and to participate in seminars and class discussions. Social problems were reported, but two-thirds of the respondents denied having had them.

Of those attending colleges other than Gallaudet College, most majored in the natural sciences. Study of a major field of concentration at college was the chief preparation for their professional careers. The only problems in a capable deaf person's preparation for professional work would seem, from the replies of these respondents, to be the selection of his college and his major. Experienced teachers know, however, that numerous emotional and social problems grow from a situation where a college student diverges excessively from the norm of his environment. It is possible that the problems which these respondents found large during their college days have dimmed with the passing of the years.

Chapter IV

ENTRY INTO CAREERS

Hᴏᴡ ᴅᴏᴇꜱ ᴀ ᴅᴇᴀꜰ ᴘᴇʀꜱᴏɴ choose a career? Is deafness the dominant factor? Is he guided into the choice by school, by parents, by friends? Is it an early or a late decision, or a developing thing throughout childhood and youth? Is job-seeking an entirely special process for a deaf person or does he encounter problems similar to those of his hearing peers with merely a little additional difficulty about communication? Does he face discrimination?

For a deaf person the problems of selecting and entering an occupation are numerous, varied and practically untouched by research. Although this study can offer few definite conclusions, it is hoped that these respondents who have met the tests of actual experience can, by their disclosures, provide cues and clues to further research.

A career provides a framework for life development. Hence the selection of an occupation compatible with one's interests, aptitudes and training is, in the words of Dubin,[6] "one of the overriding considerations in his entire life history." The deaf man's choice, however, must go beyond compatibility, competence and training. He must consider whether, once trained, he can overcome prejudice and gain acceptance—whether his ears or his skills will determine his employment opportunities.

HOW SELECTION OF OCCUPATION WAS MADE

It might seem that deaf persons, faced with all the usual problems of an occupational choice plus the need to select one in which they can anticipate acceptance, would tend by a large majority to make their selection by deliberate decision. Such is not the case, according to the present respondents. They were asked, "Did you make a deliberate choice of your kind of work, or did you get into the work more or less by chance?" In reply, forty-four (51 per cent) said that they had made their selection by choice; thirty-four (39 per cent) attributed their selection to chance and the remaining nine were uncertain.

Since there were indications of some confusion, these answers were not accepted without some qualification. An analysis of work histories resulted in shifts in fourteen cases so that the analyst's interpretation resulted in fifty-one (59 per cent) by choice and thirty-one (36 per cent) by chance with five undecided. In either case, the majority who made their selections by choice is relatively small in face of the assumption made at the start of this chapter.

There may exist in the figures a slight bias toward selection by chance due to the depression of the 1930's. When respondents were classified by age and by manner of selection of occupation, as in Table 32, a majority in each age group made their selection by choice. An exception was the group for the ages 45-54, which registered just under half for selection by choice and almost the same figure for selection by chance. This was the group who entered the labor force in the years 1929-38, when one took whatever job was available, if any.

TABLE 32
SELECTION OF OCCUPATION, BY AGE

			Age			
Manner of	*Total*		*25-34*	*35-44*	*45-54*	*55 & Up*
Selection	*Number*	*Per Cent*	*Per Cent*	*Per Cent*	*Per Cent*	*Per Cent*
By choice	51	59	76	56	48	57
By chance	31	36	19	36	44	43
Uncertain	5	6	5	8	7	
Total, per cent		101	100	100	99	100
Respondents	87		(21)	(25)	(27)	(14)

Of those respondents who made the selection by deliberate choice, a majority did so during the years of their early youth, whereas most of those who entered their profession by chance did so later in life. Table 33 shows that 63 per cent of those who decided by choice made their commitment during early childhood or adolescence. Of those who selected by chance, 55 per cent made the selection during their working careers and 23 per cent did so during their college years for a total of 78 per cent who selected their occupations after adolescence.

Of the seventeen who had selected their occupations by chance during their working careers, nine had not been graduated from

TABLE 33

SELECTION OF OCCUPATION, PERIOD OF
DECISION, BY MANNER OF SELECTION

Period of Decision	Total	Manner of Selection		
		By Choice	By Chance	Mixed
Early childhood	22	17	4	1
Adolescence	19	15	3	1
College years	20	10	7	3
During working career	23	6	17	
No answer	3	3		
Total	87	51	31	5

college; four were graduated during the depression years; two made late transfers from other employment and one took the first job available after college. The situation was summarized by a respondent who said, "When you want to eat, you're not particular."

The respondents were asked, with open-end questions, how the choice was made or how the chance had occurred. These questions were followed by probes to elicit additional factors and to classify these factors as sources of information, self-attributes or characteristics of the occupation. The replies were coded and tabulated in two ways: (1) the *first-named*—and presumably the strongest—factor alone (these data appear in Table 34) and (2) *all* factors which entered into the respondents' decisions in Table 35.

Source of information was the first-named factor most frequently

TABLE 34

SELECTION OF OCCUPATION: CHIEF FACTOR

Chief Factor	Number	Per Cent
Self-attributes:	(31)	(36)
Interest	21	24
Deafness	6	7
Aptitude	4	5
Sources of information:	(47)	(54)
School or teacher	19	22
Relative	16	18
Friend	5	6
Employer or supervisor	4	5
Other	3*	3
Characteristics of the occupation:	(9)	(10)
Opportunities	6	7
Congenial work	2	2
Challenge	1	1
Total	87	100

*One each: co-worker, employment officer, seminar or employment.

TABLE 35

SELECTION OF OCCUPATION: ALL FACTORS

Factor	Number	Per Cent
Self-attributes:		
Deafness	46	53
Aptitude	13	15
Interest	53	61
None	1	1
No answer	8	9
Respondents	(87)*	—*
Sources of information:		
School or teacher	29	33
Relative	23	26
Friend	7	8
Employer or supervisor	7	8
Other	4†	5
None		
No answer	17	20
Respondents	87	100
Characteristics of the occupation:		
Congenial work	31	36
Challenge	5	6
Opportunities	15	17
Material reward	6	7
Prestige	3	3
No answer	28	32
Respondents	(87)*	—*

*Totals exceed number of respondents and 100 per cent because of multiple answers.
†One each: co-worker, employment officer, want ads and seminar on employment.

cited in these responses; forty-seven respondents (54 per cent) chose sources of information as the chief factor in occupational selection. Among them, school personnel and relatives were the leading sources. Several respondents indicated considerable dependence on these sources of information; one respondent expressed it thus: "He (the respondent's father) talked to my technical school teacher and he thought maybe I should be a draftsman and so I'm a draftsman."

When occupational selection was analyzed in relation to *all* contributing factors (Table 35), interest in the work was the most frequently cited factor in selection; fifty-three respondents (61 per cent) cited interest as one of the factors in their decision. More than half named deafness as another factor.

Those who cited deafness as a factor stressed its limiting aspects:

Because I was given to understand that it (occupation chosen) requires a minimum of conversation with other people.

You have to think of a field where hearing is not important.

I knew I couldn't be a doctor so I thought chemistry would be almost the same field.

In bookkeeping you're permitted to work from documents and invoices, nobody bothers you or anything like that, so I thought that would be a perfect vocation for me.

Some qualified deafness as a factor, as with one respondent who said:

My deafness is a factor in everything, but it isn't the only factor. So I am a chemist because I like the work.

One attributed his selection to a common school difficulty for deaf persons:

When I was a little boy, I always had a lot of difficulty in reading to understand stories or articles, but it was easier for me to understand adding or subtracting which didn't require reading.

Deafness as a factor in the selection of occupation was further examined by analyzing other questions connected with occupational choice. (The opening question of the interview, "How did you happen to become a ——?", which was meant as an ice-breaker, often elicited an extended career history.) The questions analyzed included the opening question just mentioned and queries about (1) childhood ambitions and experiences, (2) parental occupation, (3) choice of the occupation followed and (4) other occupations considered. References to deafness in any of the replies to these questions were counted and classified in Table 36 to indicate the degree of importance attributed to deafness by the respondents.

TABLE 36

SELECTION OF OCCUPATION: DEAFNESS
AS A FACTOR, BY MANNER OF SELECTION

Deafness as a Factor	Total	By Choice	By Chance	Mixed
Major factor	39	25	11	3
Minor factor	11	5	6	
Negative factor*	7	7		
Not a factor†	8	4	4	
Not mentioned	21	9	10	2
No answer	1	1		
Total	87	51	31	5

*Selection was made in spite of respondent's knowledge that deafness might interfere with success.
†Respondents specifically denied deafness as a factor.

More than half of the respondents considered deafness to have been a factor in their career selection. Deafness was less often a factor among those whose selection was made by chance; 45 per cent did not mention deafness at any time or they denied that it influenced them in their selection. Seven (14 per cent) of those whose selections were by deliberate choice entered their professions in spite of the fact that deafness might make their progress difficult. One of these described this type of reasoning thus:

> I think it was the time Mr. —— came to college and gave a speech. His speech wasn't very enthusiastic; his speech wasn't very good. He didn't encourage people to become chemists very much. It was a little bit more discouraging. And I made up my mind there that I'd show him that the deaf could be chemists.

There seems to be some evidence that respondents who had received most of elementary and secondary education in schools for the deaf were less deterred by deafness from a desired occupation than were those who attended schools for hearing persons. Table 37 shows that, for 50 per cent of those who had attended schools for the deaf the longest, deafness was a positive factor in the selection of an occupation, i.e., influenced them to choose a certain occupation because it was more suitable for deaf people. The seven respondents who selected occupations in which they stated that they knew their deafness might be a drawback came from schools for the deaf. Of those who attended schools for hearing persons, 74 per cent considered deafness a positive factor.

A superficial conclusion may be that schools for the deaf are able to imbue confidence in one's ability to overcome the handicap. Perhaps there is an element of confidence arising from familiarity with

TABLE 37

SELECTION OF OCCUPATION: DEAFNESS AS A FACTOR, BY TYPE OF ELEMENTARY AND SECONDARY SCHOOL ATTENDED LONGEST

	Type of School Attended Longest			
Deafness as a Factor in Selection of Occupation	Schools for the Deaf		Schools for the Hearing	
	Number	Per Cent	Number	Per Cent
Positive factor	28	50	23	74
Negative factor	7	12		
Not a factor	21	37	8	26
Total	56	99	31	100

adult models who have already adjusted to their lack of hearing. There are, however, these elements to be considered as well: Those who attended public schools the longest were predominantly those who had lost their hearing later in youth (48 per cent of them were deafened after age twelve; 26 per cent between six and twelve) and hence were more aware of changes in ambitions caused by their deafness; for those who had been deaf since very early childhood, the gradual process of occupational choice may not have emphasized deafness so much because of their long familiarity with the phenomenon.

OCCUPATIONS CHOSEN

The respondents chose twenty-nine different occupations, mostly of a laboratory nature.* These occupations have been classified in seven fields (Table 38) for purposes of cross tabulation.

TABLE 38
OCCUPATIONAL FIELDS

Occupational Field	Number of Respondents
Art and architecture	8
Business	5
Chemistry	23
Engineering	25
Library work and museum work	5
Mathematics and statistics	9
Other sciences	7
Miscellaneous	5
Total	87

The large number of respondents working as chemists is understandable when it is considered that chemistry was for many years the only well-developed professional training offered at Gallaudet College, where many of the respondents were educated and that chemistry is well regarded as a career throughout the deaf community. Engineering, the field selected by the most respondents, may be thought of as an undeveloped profession for deaf persons insofar as special education is concerned. Library careers have been developed in recent years by more deaf persons than the number here shown would indicate.

---

*See Table 42 for a detailed listing of occupations of the respondents.

Motivation for the choice made was expressed by one respondent thus:

> Well, I realized the fields of business were largely out for me. In business work you are working with persons all the time. You can probably attest that this lip-reading is quite a strain. A couple of hours of it and you're pretty well played out. If I had to do that day in and day out, eight hours a day, it would be difficult.

Yet seeking the isolation of laboratory work can backfire, as it did in another instance:

> Before I was trying to get away from people, now I am trying to get to people. But here I am alone all the time and five years of it gets on my nerves. I'm in here all day from morning to night. Nobody comes in except the man who brings the mail and the janitor. . . .

Respondents were asked if they had considered occupations other than those presently followed. Sixty-two of them answered affirmatively, naming thirty occupations. These have been classified in Table 39 by the same groupings as Table 38 and by the Bureau of the Census occupational scale for occupations other than professional. The sciences (twenty-seven), teaching (sixteen) and printing (twelve) lead the other occupations considered. The sciences predominate probably because of the natural bent of the respondents. Teaching and printing were frequently mentioned probably because they are among the most widely followed occupations of deaf people and

TABLE 39

OTHER OCCUPATIONS CONSIDERED BY RESPONDENTS

Professions	Number	Other Occupations	Number
Art and architecture	5	Managers and proprietors	
Business	4	(farm)	4
Chemistry	6	Sales and kindred work	1
Clergy	2	Craftsmen, printers	12
College faculty	1	Craftsmen, other	4
Engineering	10	Other occupations considered	
Law	1	but not named	2
Library work and museum			—
work	1		23*
Mathematics and			
statistics	4		
Other sciences	11		
Teaching	16		
	61*		

*The total of 84 choices exceeds the 62 respondents who had considered other occupations because of multiple answers.

hence were well represented as occupations of the models which the respondents had observed during their youth.

THE FIRST JOB

One respondent's remark, "I wrote approximately 750 letters of application," serves to identify one of the greatest difficulties experienced by deaf people in employment, especially in professional employment—the reluctance to hire applicants who deviate from the norm.

Illustrative is this experience of a respondent:

> The personnel manager . . . wanted to know what my IQ was. He told me I must have a high IQ to have a master's degree despite the fact that I was deaf. . . . But anyway he wanted to give me a chance so he went over to talk to the chief chemist. And the chief got mad because he even brought me over . . . definitely antagonistic to hiring a deaf chemist.

This reluctance probably arises from the fear of the unknown. Deaf people are a tiny minority of the population and many people go through life without any meaningful contact with deaf persons. Hiring officials often have fears, reasonable or not, that deaf applicants may be incapable of doing the work or may have great communication difficulties or personality problems. One respondent described his reception thus:

> They didn't know what to make of me. They seemed ill at ease with me. They looked on me as a freak. My voice probably wasn't normal. They knew something was wrong with me from the way I spoke. They found out soon enough what was wrong with me. And thereafter they were friendly enough; most of them were ill-at-ease with me except for a few warm-hearted people who befriended me and are still my friends today.

Dr. B. M. Schowe,[12] retired deaf labor relations official with the Firestone Tire and Rubber Company, objects to labeling this unease discrimination (with its connotations of prejudice):

> We can use harsh terms if we like and call this "discrimination." But such a label provides no insight into its cause and cure. The fact is that successful businesses resemble a watch in some of their aspects. They are smooth-running organizations with each job carefully engineered to fit into its place and perform certain specific functions . . . the department

manager would still find it hard to imagine how one of these carefully engineered jobs could be performed without frequent conferences and the normal range of communication.

There is also the question of first impressions and here the deaf applicant meets a particularly difficult situation. Samuel A. Block,[3] then section chief with the Railroad Retirement Board, described this situation in relation to government employment:

> Whether or not an appointing officer is properly equipped to deal with handicapped applicants is of especial importance if the applicant is deaf. That is because deafness (accompanied as it usually is by impairment of the vocal organs) is *unique* among handicaps in that it is the major one which retards free communication between an appointing officer and applicant. The attitude of an appointing officer (even one with the best will) toward a deaf person, therefore, cannot help but be colored by whatever initial difficulties he has in interviewing a deaf person for a job. He is likely to be unfavorably impressed if the interview is made more difficult and awkward because of the failure of the appointing officer and the applicant to understand each other. This will not, of course, be entirely the fault of the applicant. No matter how much training in lipreading he may have received, his success in lipreading depends also upon the ability of the persons "listened to" to move their lips in a reasonably typical fashion. Moreover, no matter how well a deaf person can speak, even by the standards of the non-deaf, an appointing officer will have difficulty understanding what is being said to him if he has allowed the knowledge that it is a deaf person speaking to "condition" him against understanding.

Dr. Schowe[13] has also adverted to this unfamiliarity, pointing to the value of intervention by a third party in the application process:

> Confronted with a proposal to employ a deaf worker, the responsible official, without any reliable data to serve as a guide, is more likely than not to say, "The heck with it."
>
> Under these circumstances there are only three or four catalysts which will convert the applicant into a job holder. The responsible official may know of deaf workers on similar jobs in another plant; or there is someone in plant or office who is familiar with the deaf and will vouch for them; or else a placement officer succeeds in winning the confidence of the employer and convinces him that hiring the deaf is practical.

One respondent put into a nutshell the experience of a good many of them:

> At first when I applied there myself, the woman in the employment

office said that because of my deafness I couldn't work there, but after my grand-uncle wrote the letter, I got in.

But what was the consensus of the respondents' experiences in their initial job hunting? All were asked regarding their first full-time job, "Did you secure the job yourself or did you have help?" Fifty-six (64 per cent) of the respondents acknowledged help and thirty-one indicated they had received no help.

The fifty-six who had help were asked about the source and nature of that help; Table 40 records the replies.

It was chiefly relatives and friends who assisted the respondents in their initial job-seeking. Members of the family and friends each aided in placement for seventeen of the respondents. The friends were about equally divided between friends of the family and deaf friends of the respondent. Much of the help from these friends and relatives took the form of active participation in the job hunt; of the thirty instances of direct contact by the assisting party with the employer, twenty-three were by relatives or friends. Some of them even dominated the employment interview:

> . . . and my father talked a lot about my character and education and things like that; all I did was sit quietly like a little boy.

or, more constructively:

> . . . and my mother didn't help any more after that. I took over after the introduction to the friend.

The schools and employment agencies were more impersonal in their employment assistance. Of the eighteen respondents so helped, thirteen were only informed of the job opening or given a letter of introduction or provided intern training while at college. The latter method was described thus:

> My part-time job led to a permanent job. When I was going to —— U., I got a summer job here between school years, and when I got my degree, they offered me a permanent job.

How did the thirty-one respondents who were unaided secure their jobs? Thirteen respondents applied cold, that is, no preliminary maneuvers preceded their interviews or letters of application; eight answered advertisements, four took examinations and one applied

TABLE 40

SECURING THE FIRST JOB: SOURCE OF HELP, BY TYPE
OF HELP: RESPONDENTS WHO HAD HELP

Source of Help	Total	Type of Help by Third Party							
		Made All Arrangements	Assisted at Interview	Discussed Job With Employer	Told Employer About Respondent	Wrote Letter of Introduction	Told Respondent About Job	Other	No Answer
Relative	17	7	1	2	4	2	1		
Friend	17	5	1	2	1	2	5		1
School or teacher	13	2		1		3	3	3*	1
Employment agency	5			1	1‡		3		
Other	3	1†			1‡		1§		
No answer	1								1
Total	56	15	2	6	7	7	13	3	3

*Moved from summer to permanent employment.
†By a former supervisor in a WPA project.
‡By a recruiter.
§By another company which had rejected the respondent's application.

to a recruiter. Five respondents did not answer this question. Of the thirteen who applied cold, four did so by letter and nine in person.

It seems justifiable to assume from the preceding data that some sort of catalyst is necessary to trigger a favorable reaction to the prospect of employing a deaf person. In most cases, the catalyst was prior contact by someone other than the deaf applicant; it is only logical to assume that encomiums on the qualifications of an applicant are more readily believed when they come from a third party. In the case of the thirteen respondents who secured their positions by answering advertisements or taking examinations or applying to a recruiter, the catalyst may have been the employer's pressing need to fill the position. Even the four who applied cold by letter had the opportunity to present their qualifications before the employing official was transfixed by the shock of learning that the applicant was deaf.

In some cases, employer resistance may have been softened by the employing official's having had prior acquaintance with deaf people as co-workers, friends, relatives or neighbors. Thirteen such prior contacts had eased the way for applicants who had had no third party assistance in applying. In the fifty-six instances where the hiring officer did not have previous acquaintance with deaf people, the respondents knew of thirteen instances of other people in the firm knowing deaf persons.

The question of whether employers, supervisors or co-workers felt resistance to the idea of having a deaf worker in the laboratory, office or plant was considered. It is patently impossible to measure the inner feelings of the company officials, but the respondents' perception of resistance was sought. Respondents were asked, in relation to their first job, "So far as you know, was there open resistance to the idea of hiring you because you were deaf?" Table 41 reveals that 66 per cent of the respondents perceived no resistance to their being hired because of their deafness.

Specific cases of discrimination among those who did perceive resistance were described thus:

> They said that they had a policy that would not allow them to hire handicapped people.

> They just didn't want to have anything to do with handicapped people and another concern . . . thought it would be too dangerous because I would have to go out into the foundry.

TABLE 41

DEGREE OF RESISTANCE TO HIRING A DEAF WORKER,
AS PERCEIVED BY RESPONDENT, BY PREVIOUS ACQUAINTANCE
OF COMPANY PERSONNEL WITH DEAF PERSONS

Degree of Resistance Perceived	Total	*Previous Acquaintance of Company Personnel With Deaf Persons*		
		Acquainted with Deaf Persons	Not Acquainted With Deaf Persons	Don't Know and No Reply
Slight*	5	4	1	
Moderate†	15	5	8	2
Great‡	3		3	
No resistance	57	34	22	1
Don't know	4	1	3	
No answer	3		2	1
Total	87	44	39	4

Slight indicates any use of modifiers to minimize resistance perceived.
†*Moderate* indicates resistance but no qualifications as to extent.
‡*Great* indicates use of modifiers to emphasize resistance perceived.

Resistance was often based on, or veiled by, health or safety factors:

They told me that they were not against deaf chemists but they claimed that they had an insurance clause in their contract that was against hiring deaf people.

Sometimes the health or safety department actually overruled the hiring official:

There was a chief chemist in —— Company . . . that wanted to hire me but the medical department said they definitely wouldn't.

Sometimes the resistance took form less stringent than rejection:

I was on trial for a month. Most of the others were on trial much less than that. I think it was because they were leery of a deaf man doing the job. But when the month was up they knew I could do the work.

Some who reported no resistance qualified their statements:

There wasn't any resistance but they were watching me like a hawk to see how I was doing.

No, it was wartime and they were more than glad to take someone who had two hands and was willing to work.

They did not look on me as deaf so much. It wasn't so important at that level of work. I was a clerk; I could read the lips. They could give me instructions almost as easily as they could give people of normal hearing.

Resistance was overcome in some places, as with the notorious former requirement of the United States Civil Service Commission that applicants be able to hear an ordinary tone of voice at a distance of fifteen feet:

> I wanted to take the Federal Civil Service examination to become a professional statistician . . . But it (the announcement) had a little clause in it that said the examination was not offered to people who could not hear a whisper at fifteen feet. We talked the matter over with my superior and he went with us to the Civil Service Commission and got in to see the chief medical officer who was responsible for that particular restriction and asked him why. You don't have to hear to compute a few statistics. The medical officer said that clause was in because the Civil Service Commission felt that there would be no jobs open to a deaf person that most persons want to talk to the statistician personally. That's very natural but since my superior had already asked about that, there was evidence that there would be some openings for deaf persons.

That these difficulties were perceived by persons other than disappointed applicants is attested by the following statement of a colleague:

> He was originally hired on the basis of his friendship with the fellow next door here. . . . He had a devil of a time getting him in here, for a fact, but of course once he got in there was no problem at all. Never any question about him being at the top of the list of people in his category.

Fortunately, attitudes of rejection are not universal and honest doubts can be resolved with the proper approach. Most of the respondents showed an awareness of the need for, (1) a careful selection of a suitable occupation and (2) a carefully planned job-hunting campaign. In most cases the aid of a third party would be needed to reduce the barriers created by unfamiliarity with deaf peoples' abilities.

SUMMARY

Occupational choices were made by roughly equal proportions of the respondents in each of the four periods used for analysis: childhood, adolescence, college years and working period. Contrary to logical expectation, the selection was not always made deliberately and deafness was not necessarily the first factor in all selections. Sources of information, chiefly relatives and friends, were the factors first cited by most of the respondents as influencing their selections. Deafness was among the influences cited by over half of the respondents but only six of them gave it precedence. Of self-attributes, interest in the occupation had the strongest influence upon their selection. Twenty-nine different occupations were chosen, most of them in laboratories.

The chief problem in securing the first job was discrimination, yet only a third of the respondents reported that they actually were discriminated against. In breaking down barriers to employment, a third person was a catalyst for fifty-six of the job applicants. Probably the greatest single difficulty the respondents met in their working lives was breaking the ice on their first job application.

Chapter V

OCCUPATIONS AND ECONOMIC POSITION

Very little definitive information about the general occupational patterns of deaf people is known. Because they are a small minority of the population and a very difficult group to define or to discover, statistical analyses in general studies and surveys have tended to disregard deaf people. Where hearing handicap was a matter of interest, the tendency in the past has been to lump together the hard-of-hearing and the deaf subjects, actually disparate groups. Two fairly comprehensive studies have been made of occupational conditions of deaf persons: Elise Martens'[10] survey made during the depression and the previously cited survey by Bigman and Lunde, a more recent and more extensive study.

Neither study can be said to reflect accurately the characteristics of the total deaf population because they are not representative samples. An ideal representation is practically impossible to achieve because of the lack of benchmark census data on the deaf population. The Martens study, in addition to this shortcoming, was made during the great depression, hardly a representative economic period. In comparing the data of *The Survey of Occupational Conditions Among the Deaf*,[2] readers are asked to bear in mind that although this is the largest and best analyzed occupational study of deaf people to date, the authors stated, "There is reason to believe that the survey group may underrepresent the age groups under twenty and over sixty, women, Negroes and persons at the lowest economic level."

The Bigman-Lunde survey covered 10,101 deaf persons and showed broadly the following occupational conditions among the groups.

1. A heavy concentration in the skilled and semi-skilled manual occupations and relatively few professional and sales workers.
2. A wide range of 400 occupations. (The authors commented, "There does not seem to be much of a limit to what *some* deaf persons can do.")

3. An average income of $3,564 per year, higher than that of the general population ($2,818). When incomes were compared at each occupational level, however, that of the deaf respondents was lower than that of the general population.
4. Relatively little occupational mobility among the group.
5. Some slight evidence for the conclusion that the age at which deafness occurred influences occupational achievement.
6. Lipreading ability is related to occupational and income levels and also (negatively) to job stability.

There are, in addition, certain experiences and observations in regard to high level employment of deaf people which have a general acceptance among deaf people themselves. Employers often are dubious about employing deaf people, probably doubting their capacities and their ability to by-pass communication blocks and possibly reacting negatively to abnormality. Deaf individuals have succeeded in occupations where hearing, at first glance, seems to be essential, such as writing poetry, public relations, electronics, auto repair. Deaf persons who are job-oriented seem to carry the attitude of concentration on their jobs further than do other people, possibly because they have been told that they must over-compensate for their handicap. There is a ceiling on advancement at or near the level where frequent contacts with persons who hear becomes essential.

OCCUPATIONS FOLLOWED

Twenty-nine occupations were reported by the eighty-seven respondents in this study. The occupations are listed in Table 42.

A considerable variety of occupations were represented, but the impression of variety may be misleading. Almost three-fourths of the respondents were in scientific pursuits. Engineering (twenty-five) and chemistry (twenty-three) drew over half of them and mathematics and other sciences claimed sixteen. The remaining twenty respondents were distributed among twelve occupations. All but a few respondents were in laboratory, workroom or desk positions which required minimal contact with the public.

The women in the group had desk jobs, mainly in libraries and museums. This does not necessarily mean that there are no deaf women in laboratories; there have been deaf women chemists, for example, but the laboratory professions do not seem to attract many deaf women. The classification followed in the table was that of the Bureau of the Census.[4]

The Survey of Occupational Conditions Among the Deaf indicated that age of occurrence of deafness might have influenced the occupations followed. Among the present respondents, as shown in Table 43, the proportion of early deafened respondents employed in the

TABLE 42

OCCUPATIONS OF RESPONDENTS, BY SEX

Occupations	Total	Sex Male	Female
Business:	(5)	(4)	(1)
Accountants	4*	3	1
Not classified	1	1	
Art and Architecture:	(8)	(7)	(1)
Architects	1	1	
Artists	3	2	1
Architectural draftsmen	4	4	
Chemistry:	(23)	(23)	
Chemists	23	23	
Engineering:	(25)	(25)	
Aeronautical engineers	3	3	
Designers	2	2	
Draftsmen	6†	6	
Civil engineers	4	4	
Industrial engineers	2	2	
Mechanical engineers	2	2	
Metal engineers, metallurgists	2	2	
Surveyors	1	1	
Engineers not otherwise classified	3	3	
Library work and museum work:	(5)	(1)	(4)
Librarians	2	1	1
Museum workers	3		3
Mathematics and statistics:	(9)	(8)	(1)
Mathematicians	4	4	
Statisticians and actuaries	5	4	1
Other sciences:	(7)	(7)	
Agricultural scientists	1	1	
Biological scientists	3	3	
Physicists	1	1	
Miscellaneous natural scientists	2	2	
Miscellaneous:	(5)	(4)	(1)
Editors and reporters (public relations)	1	1	
Lawyers and judges	1	1	
Photographers	1		1
Social and welfare workers	1	1	
Technicians, medical and dental	1	1	
Total	87	79	8

*Includes one controller.
†Includes 3 cartographic draftsmen.

sciences is 58 per cent, compared to 65 per cent of those employed in other occupations who were deafened before age six. Art and architecture, library work and museum work had high proportions of those deafened before age six, but the numbers in each occupational group were too small to justify within-group conclusions.

It is encouraging to note that deaf-born respondents were employed in all occupational groups except business and miscellaneous. There is, it seems, no need for an otherwise well-endowed person who was born deaf to doubt his ability to function in the professions covered in this study.

TABLE 43

OCCUPATIONAL CLASSIFICATION,
BY AGE OF OCCURRENCE OF DEAFNESS

| | | Age of Occurrence of Deafness | | |
Occupational Classification	*Total*	*Born Deaf*	*Under 6 Years*	*Over 6 Years*
Art and architecture	8	5	2	1
Business	5		2	3
Chemistry	23	8	6	9
Engineering	25	8	6	11
Library work and museum work	5	2	2	1
Mathematics and statistics	9	2	2	5
Other sciences	7	1	4	2
Miscellaneous	5		2	3
Total	87	26	26	35

Bigman and Lunde found lipreading ability to be related to occupational level. Tables 44 and 45 indicate no especial concentration of the higher speech skills in any single occupational grouping except in library work and museum work where the total number of respondents was too small to be statistically significant. The highest lipreading ability was possessed by a very small proportion in every group except the miscellaneous. It would seem that while moderate skill in the speech arts was to be found among deaf workers in most of the professions covered, optimum skill was not essential to their professional employment. Among the respondents employed in the sciences, 41 per cent rated themselves as having the best speech and 16 per cent, top quality lipreading; respondents in occupations other than sciences numbered 48 and 35 percent, respectively, in the top categories of speech skills.

TABLE 44

OCCUPATIONAL CLASSIFICATION, BY EXPRESSIVE SPEECH SKILLS, AS PERCEIVED BY RESPONDENTS

Occupational Classification	Total	Expressive Speech Skills—Associates Understand				
		Practically All Said	Almost Everything	Occasional Word	Never Speak	Other
Art and architecture	8	1	4	2	1	
Business	5	2	1	2		
Chemistry	23	12	8	1		2*
Engineering	25	10	8	6	1	
Library work and museum work	5	4				1†
Mathematics and statistics	9	2	3	3	1	
Other sciences	7	2	4	1		
Miscellaneous	5	4	1			
Total	87	37	29	15	3	3

*Length of acquaintance affects understanding, 1; no answer, 1.
†Length of acquaintance affects understanding.

TABLE 45

OCCUPATIONAL CLASSIFICATION, BY RECEPTIVE SPEECH SKILLS, AS PERCEIVED BY RESPONDENTS

Occupational Classification	Total	Receptive Speech Skills—Respondent Understands				
		Almost Everything	Short Conversations	Short Simple Sentences	Occasional Word	No Answer
Art and architecture	8	1	4		2	1
Business	5	1	3	1		
Chemistry	23	5	11	6		1
Engineering	25	3	12	6	4	
Library work and museum work	5	2	2	1		
Mathematics and statistics	9	1	1	5	2	
Other sciences	7	1	3		3	
Miscellaneous	5	4	1			
Total	87	18	37	19	11	2

SUITABILITY OF OCCUPATIONS

How do the respondents feel about their occupations in relation to their deafness? In this respect, do they consider themselves to be engaged in occupations appropriate to deaf people? They were asked, "Do you think your profession is well suited to deaf persons?" Table 46 reveals that only four of the eighty-seven respondents considered their occupations unsuited to deaf persons. This judgment by no means indicated that these four respondents were discontented with their positions; all four were eminently successful and took satisfaction in the fact. They recognized, however, that their professions—law, public relations, museum work and land surveying and real estate— required public contacts and much communication, making them less accessible to deaf workers. The museum worker, very happy in her own career, had not experienced this drawback greatly herself but projected an observed trend in museum work requiring experts in any field to go out and meet the public in order better to disseminate the information they had gathered. This trend, she felt, would make advancement in museum work more difficult for deaf persons in future years.

Of the eighty-one respondents who said that their professions were suited to deaf people, forty-three qualified their replies to the effect that suitability did not extend to average deaf workers. Thirty-seven of the forty-three said that extra skill and brains or effort were required and six cited the need for exceptional speech skills. Five respondents called attention to the fact that advancement in their fields was limited by the communication factor.

Respondents were asked to tell what it was about their occupations that made them suitable for deaf persons. The outstanding characteristic of occupations deemed suitable for deaf persons was, as might be expected, the absence of need for frequent oral communication (expressed as "little communication involved" or "work requiring a minimum of distraction"). Sixty of the seventy-seven respondents answering this question cited this characteristic; forty-six of the sixty were employed in the sciences. The remainder of the replies dealt with the general attractiveness of their careers in terms of congenial work, material rewards, challenge and advancement.

TABLE 46

SUITABILITY OF OCCUPATION, BY OCCUPATIONAL GROUP

Suitability of Occupation	Total	Occupational Groups							
		Business	Art and Architecture	Chemistry	Engineering	Library and Museum Work	Mathematics and Statistics	Other Sciences	Miscellaneous
Suitable	33	2	1	12	7	3	5	2	1
Suitable, but requires brain, skill, interest	37	3	4	8	13	1	4	4	
Suitable, but requires speech skills	6			2	2			1	1
Suitable, but advancement limited	5	2		1	1				1
Unsuitable	4				1	1			2
No answer	2	1			1				
Total	87	8	5	23	25	5	9	7	5

The respondents were also asked what there was about deaf people themselves that made them suited to the occupations. Freedom from distraction due to noise was the only characteristic cited as being peculiar to deaf people; twenty-five respondents gave this explanation. An almost equal number stated that deafness was not a help in their occupations. Twenty-seven did not answer this question and a few (seven) cited alertness and patience, which are characteristics not unique to deaf people.

Suitability of occupation could also be viewed through the eyes of hearing co-workers. If they thought their deaf co-workers were handling their jobs effectively, it is reasonable to suppose that they would be equally receptive to another similarly endowed deaf worker. Seventy-nine hearing workers said that their deaf colleagues were doing as well as (twenty-three) or better than (fifty-six), other co-workers in their jobs. Only three respondents were rated as not doing as well.

As the colleagues saw it, their favorable views were shared by other hearing co-workers. When asked what the attitudes of business associates would be toward employing a person like the respondent, forty-five colleagues opined that co-workers would be favorable and twenty-six felt that co-workers would be strongly favorable. Only three colleagues perceived possible unfavorable attitudes; seven anticipated neutral reactions; three did not know and three did not answer.

The question of how people would react to the hiring of more deaf workers elicited a less enthusiastic response. Only nineteen said that attitudes of co-workers would be favorable; thirty-nine anticipated neutrality; six expected unfavorable reaction; twenty-three did not reply. This lack of enthusiasm may have arisen from reluctance to commit the organization, since few of the colleagues were involved in selection of personnel.

A general conclusion in the matter of suitable occupations might be that the choice is an individual matter, although the element of communication enters the picture strongly. As a rule, a laboratory or a desk job is preferable for a deaf person, but if ingenuity, aggressiveness and communication skills are strong, the worker's choice can be broad, even into occupations where communication plays a large role—sales, for example. Generally, warm acceptance by co-workers may be anticipated once the ice of job entry has been broken.

EMPLOYERS

A large variety of business firms, research groups and government agencies were included among the fifty-nine employers of the respondents. The United States Government employed far more of them (twenty-four) than did any other employer. Employing three each were Firestone Tire and Rubber Company, the Hispanic Society of America and North American Aviation; employers of two were General Dynamics and United States Steel Company Research Center. A full list of employers is given in Appendix C.

INCOME

These deaf persons in professional occupations enjoyed a high level of income. In fact, their median income from salaries (Table 47) was $7,615, as compared to $7,036 for salaried professional workers in the United States in 1960.[15] There is, however, an upward bias in the data for the respondent group in that those with incomes below $4,000 were excluded and the age level was twenty-five and up, whereas the data for the general population covers all income levels and ages fourteen and over. Also, the respondent group excluded teachers and ministers, whose salaries might tend to pull the median downward.

As is found in practically all other comparisons of income by sex, the male respondent received the better wages. In the present case, the median salary for men was $7,920; that for women, about $5,000.

How did the occupational groups compare among themselves in earning potential for deaf workers? Table 48 presents income of

TABLE 47

INCOME FROM WAGES AND SALARIES: RESPONDENTS
AND GENERAL POPULATION (PROFESSIONAL)

| Wages and Salaries | Respondents | | | | General Population Professionals[15] (1960) Per Cent |
| | Total | | Male | Female | |
	Number	Per Cent			
Under $4,000					17.7
4,000- 5,999	23	26	16	7	23.6
6,000- 7,999	26	30	25	1	27.0
8,000- 9,999	27	31	27		14.2
10,000-11,999	4	5	4		17.4
12,000 and over	7	8	7		
Total	87	100	79	8	99.9

TABLE 48
INCOME FROM SALARIES, BY OCCUPATIONAL GROUP

Occupational Classification	Total	$4,000 -5,999	$6,000 -7,999	$8,000 -9,999	$10,000 -11,999	$12,000 and over
Art and architecture	8	3	3	1	—	1
Business	5	3	—	1	1	—
Chemistry	23	3	9	10	—	1
Engineering	25	5	5	11	—	4
Library work and museum work	5	5	—	—	—	—
Mathematics and statistics	9	3	3	2	—	1
Other sciences	7	1	4	1	1	—
Miscellaneous	5	—	2	1	2	—
Total	87	23	26	27	4	7

respondents by occupational groups. Of these, it would seem that librarians and museum workers were the lowest paid, all five of them having received salaries below the median group ($6,000-$7,999). Engineers and miscellaneous professional workers received the best salaries.

Actually, comparison of the groups is of little value because of the small numbers. Somewhat more acceptable is the contrast between the sciences and all other professions. If $7,999, the top salary of the median group, be taken as a dividing point, 48 per cent of the scientists earned higher salaries as compared to 30 per cent of the other professionals.

As might be expected, incomes tended to peak for the respondents at the middle years. By age, salaries were distributed as shown in Table 49. Of those earning $8,000 or over 79 per cent were in the age group 35-54 years. Narrowing the peak years somewhat, 63 per cent of the respondents at ages 45-54 were earning salaries of over $8,000 a year.

None of the salaries were in exceptionally high brackets, however. Two respondents reported incomes of over $20,000, but both of these were holding more than one job.

TABLE 49

INCOME FROM SALARIES, BY AGE

		Age (in Years)			
Income	Total	Below 35	35-44	45-54	Over 55
Under $8,000	49	17	12	10	10
Over $8,000	38	4	13	17	4
Total	87	21	25	27	14

Again taking $8,000 as the middle point, Table 50 indicates a better income for those who used speech most frequently in their communication with business associates. Of those who earned $8,000 or more, 71 per cent used speech to communicate to business associates while only 57 per cent of those receiving under $8,000 did so. The proportions were closer in the case of lipreading; 58 per cent of the respondents receiving $8,000 and over and 53 per cent of those receiving under $8,000 used that means. Similar proportions existed for *skill* in speech and lipreading.

Proficiency in speech can be of cash value in professional work, it

TABLE 50

SALARY LEVELS, BY MEANS OF COMMUNICATION
MOST FREQUENTLY USED WITH HEARING PERSONS

Means of Communication	Total Number	Total Per Cent	Salary Levels Under $8,000 Number	Salary Levels Under $8,000 Per Cent	$8,000 and Over Number	$8,000 and Over Per Cent
Expressive:						
Oral	55	63	28	57	27	71
Written	30	34	19	39	11	29
Manual	2	2	2	4		
Total	87	99	49	100	38	100
Receptive:						
Oral	48	55	26	53	22	58
Written	35	40	21	43	14	37
Manual	4	5	2	4	2	5
Total	87	100	49	100	38	100

would seem from Table 51. Of those respondents whose income was
$8,000 and over, more than half had speech adequate for practically
all their conversational needs, whereas those with minimal ability to
speak comprised but 8 per cent of the higher income group. The
situation was somewhat different for lipreading. Although a slightly
larger percentage of the higher income group than that of the respondents earning below $8,000 had top lipreading skill, yet less
than one out of four in either group could understand almost every-

TABLE 51

INCOME FROM SALARIES, BY SPEECH SKILLS

Speech Skills	Income Under $8,000 Per Cent	Income $8,000 and Over Per Cent
Expressive—associates understood:		
Practically all said	33	55
Almost everything said	31	37
Occasional word or two	27	5
Other	8	3*
No answer	2	—
Total	101	100
Receptive—respondent understood:		
Almost everything said	18	24
Short conversation	43	42
Short, simple sentences	20	24
Occasional word or two	16	8
No answer	2	3
Total	99	101

*Respondent never spoke, 1; understanding varied with length of acquaintance, 2.

thing said. About 42 per cent of both groups could understand a short conversation, probably adequate for most of the casual business encounters. About one-fourth of each group had what might be called catch-as-catch-can lipreading skill; that is, they could understand a word or two or a short sentence but could not conduct an extended conversation orally.

Age of occurrence of deafness seems, from Table 52, to have some relation to income. Of the respondents earning below $8,000, thirty-six (74 per cent) had lost their hearing prior to age six, whereas twenty-two (58 per cent) of those who earned $8,000 and over had lost their hearing after age six. Ease of speech, early learning patterns, type of school attended and ease of association are probably concomitant factors here.

TABLE 52

INCOME FROM SALARIES, BY AGE OF OCCURENCE OF DEAFNESS

Age of Occurrence of Deafness	Total	Income	
		Under $8,000	$8,000 and Over
Born deaf	27	16	11
Less than 2	11	11	
2 and less than 3	5	3	2
3 and less than 6	9	6	3
6 and less than 12	16	7	9
12 and less than 15	11	3	8
15 and over	7	2	5
Age unknown	1	1	
Total	87	49	38

As was brought out in Chapter III, the respondents' salaries tend to rise as educational level rises. Of those with graduate degrees, 64 per cent earned $8,000 and over; of those with bachelor's degrees, 39 per cent; those with no degree, 35 per cent.

Another interesting relationship between education and earning power is suggested by Table 53, in which income is distributed by type of school attended the longest.

Among the high-salaried group, there was an evident preponderance of respondents who attended public schools the longest. There were many variables involved in this situation. Respondents who attended public schools the longest included a large proportion of persons whose deafness had occurred in later years, whose language and learning were stimulated earlier and more broadly and whose

TABLE 53

INCOME BY SALARIES,
BY TYPE OF SCHOOL ATTENDED LONGEST

Type of School	Total	Income				
		$4000-5,999	$6,000-7,999	$8,000-9,999	$10,000-11,999	$12,000 and over
Schools for the deaf:						
Residential:						
Public*	30	9	11	9	1	1
Private	10	7	3			
Day (Public):						
School*	11	1	3	3	1	3
Class†	4		2	2		
Schools for the hearing:						
Public	26	6	5	10	2	3
Private	4		1	2		
Other	2		1‡	1§	1	
Total	87	23	26	27	4	7

*Had own building for use of deaf pupils only.
†Shared building with regular school.
‡Five years in private residential and five years in day schools for deaf children.
§Six years in public and six years in private day schools for hearing children.

culture patterns and drives were probably more similar to those of persons who hear. The assumption from those facts would seem to be that the road to higher income was better paved for them because their life patterns more nearly resembled those of hearing persons. There is also a thesis that the populations in schools for the deaf are selective, that people high on the socioeconomic scale tend to reject the public residential school for the deaf because it is free and therefore inferior *per se* (shades of Veblen!). This thesis does not appear to be valid for the very limited population studied here, for all ten respondents who attended private residential schools (supposedly acceptable to the Brahmins) were employed at the time interviewed in the below-$8,000 class. Others have argued that because the child can be at home every day the day schools are better than residential schools. With deaf children, this question may be moot because the emotional factors entering into the parent-deaf child relationship may weigh the scales against day school arrangements. There are also two other possible factors in the school situations: (1) Residential schools for deaf children have traditionally given greater emphasis to vocational training than do the public schools, a policy not conducive to education for professional pursuits, and (2) the public schools operate in a more competitive milieu, which may favorably affect the quality of their efforts.

Income level also varies as the educational level. Of those respondents who had a master's or a doctor's degree, 64 per cent earned $8,000 or over; of those with a bachelor's degree, 39 per cent were in the $8,000 or over category. Table 30 contains data on income level by highest educational level attained.

SUMMARY

Among the twenty-nine occupations in which the respondents were employed the sciences were predominant. Chemistry drew twenty-three of them; engineering, twenty-five; mathematics and statistics, eight; other sciences, seven. Other occupations included art and architecture, seven; business, five, and one each in journalism, law, photography, social and welfare work and dental technology. Almost 90 per cent of the respondents said that their occupations were well suited to deaf workers.

Incomes of these workers were comparable to those of other professional people, their median income being somewhat higher than that of the general professional population of the United States. The scientists tended to have higher salaries than other professionals among the respondents. Speech skills, age of occurrence of deafness and extent of educational attainment varied as did income.

Chapter VI

ON-THE-JOB PROBLEMS

COMMUNICATION

IT IS A TRUISM to say that the basis of a deaf worker's on-the-job problems is communication. Like most truisms, it oversimplifies matters. The oversimplification seems to operate in two directions: (1) Communication difficulties, *per se,* are often exaggerated and fairly effective substitutes for oral communication are disregarded; (2) the pervasive nature of communication problems and their side effects may be overlooked on the one hand, or ludicrously exaggerated on the other.

Examples of the pervasiveness of communication problems are seen in the extent of a deaf person's participation in the organization's grapevine, the public relations aspect of positions at higher levels, stereotypes in the minds of people with whom the deaf person must deal, emotional friction and the like.

The attitudes encountered by these deaf job seekers (Chapter IV) showed that many employers had strong doubts about deaf people being able to communicate sufficiently to hold any job. However, actual difficulties in communication analyzed in Chapter II contradicted such a pessimistic view. There it was shown that a large majority of the respondents used speech in their business contacts for both expression and reception and that a large number of those who used writing as a first means also used speech as a second means. The replies further showed that a majority used speech and lipreading with skill. These reports of the respondents were supported by separate evaluations by their hearing colleagues who rated the deaf workers' speech skills higher than did the deaf respondents themselves.

The optimistic outlook above should not be taken to indicate that these respondents and other deaf persons meet no problems in face-to-face communication once they have learned to speak and read

[88]

the lips. Misunderstandings may still arise due to mispronunciation and overarticulation by the deaf person and to exaggerated mouth movements by the hearing person. Other difficulties are presented by the environment and the situation in which the deaf person must function. These include, for speech, adjusting vocal volume appropriately to the noise level of the surroundings and achieving suitable tone and emphasis for the subject under discussion; for lipreading, the quality of light, the physiognomy and personality of the speaker and the number of cues presented are important factors. Even in face-to-face communication, there are situational problems of the number of persons present, the purpose of the gathering, the amount of movement, etc. Nevertheless, the respondents and their colleagues have shown that, given a little ingenuity, patience and accommodation on both sides, such problems are manageable. In other communication situations, the problems are even more difficult though not insuperable.

The Telephone

Telephoning is the most obvious of these other difficult situations. A deaf person's communication is necessarily dependent upon *seeing* the individual with whom he communicates, be it for lipreading, for sign language or for writing. Vision is cut off when a telephone is used, and hence it may seem at first that there is no possible approach to the use of a telephone by a deaf person. How then, it may be wondered, was the telephone managed by the forty-six respondents who said that the use of the telephone was part of their jobs? Some did not even attempt personal use of the telephone. Eight respondents said that they left the telephoning chore to a third person; in regard to this method, one respondent said

> Well, actually I think it has forced me to do things that many of the other people who do hear should do and that is to do less telephoning themselves and let their secretaries do the work.

Some participated a bit more, staying with the third party at the telephone, receiving the message there and sending replies through the third party as needed. Thirty-two respondents used this method, twenty-three telling the third party by written communication and nine doing so orally. Facilitating these methods were the care with which the deaf person prepared his message, his ability to anticipate replies and the third party's ability to submerge self in the task of serving as an ear.

Six respondents who had suitable speech had devised means to undertake the transmission part of the task themselves, with the third party simply receiving. Their ingenuity deserves consideration. They were able to control the conversation quite well in this way. There were variations in the manner in which the third party transmitted the message to the deaf person as described below (italics supplied in all cases):

> My secretary *spells to me* (on her hands) and I reply orally. (The respondent has an extension phone; the secretary cradles the telephone on her shoulder so that both hands are free.)

> (*Told by secretary*) Then the man at the other end of the telephone will tell me what business he wants to transact with Mr. (Respondent) over the telephone, so I will *write it down* quickly and then I'll pass the telephone over to Mr. (Respondent) and put on my headset so I am free to write and use both hands. And then Mr. (Respondent) will talk to the man and then the man at the other end will undoubtedly have some further questions so he will tell them to me and I will jot them down quickly and Mr. (Respondent) will continue and that is the way it goes back and forth, on and on, and it works out very well. . . . In other words, we carry on a three-way conversation.

> The phone was connected for a signal light and whenever the phone rings, I pick up the phone and say, "Hold the line a minute, please." However, my secretary is usually available and she answers the phone; she in turn indicates verbally that the call is for me. I pick up the tie-in phone and my secretary *repeats (orally) the message* of the caller at the same time that the caller is speaking.

One respondent did not use a signal light, but:

> When Mr. —— is gone, I usually keep an arm resting on the phone. When it rings, I answer, "Just a moment, please," then call in someone to take the message.

Another respondent emphasized the part played by the person assisting:

> She's very good at synthesizing; not everyone can do that. She has a very important skill; she can give me the weight and tone of the conversation.

Negative reactions in the same direction were:

> There are many things that a third person can't feel. The other person's emotional feeling. If he's suggesting something, you'll say "Yes" or "No," but you don't get the reaction—whether he's anxious or pleased, disgusted or what.

> And for my job I think there are times when people would rather talk to me directly. Sometimes I have to call the person again because I find that the third party had the information all wrong.

The forty-six respondents were asked how well their methods of using the telephone worked. Nineteen felt that the method served them relatively well, although five of these said flatly "as well" as doing it themselves. The six who spoke themselves and had a third party to listen were all more or less satisfied. Feeling that their method was not as good were twenty-one respondents.

A compensation:

> Well, of course, using the telephone myself would be easier, yet if I could hear and use it myself, I wouldn't have such a complete telephone record, which is extremely useful.

A different view:

> Well, you can't beat being able to pick up the phone and use it yourself. I can see the advantage in that but we realize that we are deaf and know that we are limited in those things.

The forty-six respondents were asked who assisted the most in their telephoning; nineteen named subordinates; seventeen, peers; four, superiors; five, any one handy and one did not answer.

When colleagues were asked how telephone callers reacted to the respondents' deafness, six said that deafness had been found a limitation; thirteen said phoning was not required; two did not know and sixty-six said that no resistance was shown by callers. All colleagues were asked this question regardless of whether the use of a telephone was part of the respondent's job. Most deaf persons do make use of the telephone—for occasional personal messages at least.

Many of the respondents spoke of the necessity of being gracious about their dependence on a third party in telephoning. One who used the neighborhood drug store clerk or manager spoke of buying something as a gesture of appreciation. Another said, "I would say that the greatest problem for deaf people is to get other people to help them *and like it.*"*

The Conference

The conference was a problem less easily solved than the telephone. Reactions to questions about conferences ranged from one respondent who said "I am so lost as to what goes on in conferences that I am more or less left out," to the one who had a secretary able to put the conversation instantly into the sign language. In general, a third party assisted.

> One of them takes notes which are later rephrased into minutes of the meeting. Those notes not only enable me to keep up with what is being said but also permit me to take a very active part in the discussion. I am not as dependent on those notes taken at those meetings as I was on notes taken by my companions in high school or college class. Here I'm too familiar with the subject matter. I am more frequently a spokesman.

The same respondent, in reply to a question whether he read the lips of the participants, replied:

> I do, some of them. They have been my co-workers for many years. . . . Some of them speak very plainly and are easy to understand. . . . But there are others, particularly one man who is foreign-born, whom I have the greatest difficulty in understanding. The more he tries, the harder it is because he tends to exaggerate his lip movements in the wrong way.

This respondent was speaking about relatively small conferences of his division. At staff meetings in the chief executive's office, which he sometimes attended, the situation was more difficult:

> First of all, there is a much larger group there. Second, the conversational gambit is shifted back and forth very rapidly. They spend a varying amount of time on each subject and it is difficult to follow, very difficult. That's why I go only because I want to make sure that this

---

*Two aids for deaf people in communication over a distance have been developed at the San Fernando Valley (California) State College. One is an adaptation of the telewriter, previously used chiefly in business firms. The other is an electronic device which records noise when held against a telephone receiver. With this latter device, leading questions and an ingenious answering code enable a deaf person who can speak to use a telephone to a considerable extent without third party assistance.

office is properly represented as far as our position is concerned. But in order to get anything out of it, I must take someone along who takes notes for me.

Even with a note-taker, the information is secondhand and there is a time lag which can prove embarrassing, as was expressed by another respondent:

> If the meeting is going very fast, then I sometimes don't get my thoughts in without pulling the conference back to what they had just about finished discussing a minute or two earlier.

One of the more realistic impressions was contributed by a respondent who had his secretary trained to interpret into the sign language for him in numerous situations:

> I take part in the discussion about as much as anyone there. . . . It's my program they're talking about, and I have to take the initiative; I have to push it. . . . In my early days I rejected assistance. . . . I went to meetings with about twenty people sitting around the table. Very difficult situation and I tried to read lips and I could not do it very well. . . . Well, everything was fine until one time, maybe about the sixth or seventh meeting, they asked me something and I said, "Yes," and I didn't even know what they were talking about and it was in connection with an assignment. So I told my boss, "After this, if it is important enough, you send someone who can hear." . . . Later, now, at all these meetings I have my interpreter, my secretary or my assistant or one of my colleagues who can fingerspell.

The foregoing comments are typical of reactions by those respondents who did take part in conferences. Two facts seem to stand out here: (1) Lipreading is a tool of limited use, effective only in the small group where a flow of conversation is slow or controllable. Even there, the turn of a head or a carelessly placed hand will cut the deaf person off. (2) A third party taking notes gives secondhand information and creates a time lag. Accommodation by others is essential to the success of a deaf person's participation, however limited, in a conference.

That fifty-one of the respondents did take part in conferences, then, is a tribute to the cooperative spirit of their co-workers and a measure of the respect the deaf workers had earned. Of these fifty-one respondents, twenty attended conferences more often than once a month; of them it may be said that the conference was more or less a working tool. Three of these people were in positions in which they conferred daily.

Various methods of getting the drift of the meeting were used: sixteen mentioned a third party who took notes; twelve used lipreading; eight read the lips of a third party; five had someone explain the results after the conference and fill them in on what had been missed; three were provided beforehand with an agenda of the meeting; three had interpreters into the sign language; one depended on visual aids and three did not answer.

The means of expressive communication used was of some significance in conference situations. Of the fifty-one who did attend conferences, 73 per cent used speech frequently at work and 65 per cent used lipreading, whereas for the thirty-six who did not attend conferences, the division was almost equal between the oral and non-oral means of communication. Almost half of those attending conferences rated themselves at the top of the scale for speech, but only 22 per cent rated themselves at the top for lipreading.

Of course, just being present at a conference is not of particular significance; one must participate. Respondents were asked in this regard: "Which of these statements best describes your activity at a conference?" They were then handed a card containing the following statements:

1. Sit there and try to look interested.
2. Speak up when I have something of especial importance to say.
3. Take part in the discussion about as much as anyone there.
4. None of these: I *(space for comment)*.

Of the fifty-one respondents who had participated in conferences, twenty-six spoke up when necessary; eleven took part in the discussion as much as anyone there; nine attended but did not take part; two merely answered direct questions about their work; one participated somewhat less than other conferees due to delays from written transcription of the discussion and two did not answer.

Colleagues were also asked how the respondents functioned in a conference. Methods of assistance are shown in Table 54.

In the opinion of colleagues, almost half of the fifty-one respondents were aided at conferences by a person or some kind of tool. Only nine received no aid, depending, it may be supposed, on lipreading and possibly taking no active part.

TABLE 54

HOW RESPONDENTS FUNCTIONED AT GROUP
CONFERENCES, AS PERCEIVED BY COLLEAGUES

How Respondent Functioned	Number
Was aided by a person*	19
Was aided by an inanimate tool[†]	3
Was aided by a person and a tool	1
Received no external aid	9
Got along well; no method named	6
Did not get along well	4
Attendance was not required	6
Did not know	2
No answer	1
Total	51

*Person took notes or repeated gist to respondent.
†Agenda, blackboard, slides.

Some colleagues showed considerable perception of the problems created for deaf persons by group conferences. Two comments are of especial interest:

> We allow him to sit in on any group conferences, but we also approach him before the group conference and give him a brief outline so he'll know what is going to be discussed. In this way he doesn't go in cold as the other employees do. This takes a very few minutes. I would say that in five minutes you could give him an hour's conference, the basic things that are going to be discussed. Then he's allowed to sit in and then we go back and explain fully. This follow-up is more or less to be sure he got the true picture more than just explaining because he seems to feel the grasp from this small preliminary agenda, you might call it, of the conference. . . . It works out very well.

> There (in a free flowing meeting of sixty persons) the matter of breaking in when the deaf person has something to say is difficult in a group which interrupts itself all the time. Three or four people talk and it is hard to muster the courage to just yell out and say, "Look, I want to say something." . . . The difficulty of timing is something again, sometimes the remark that he wants to add has been clouded because the group has changed the subject so fast . . . I think I would like to say this: That the quality of that participation, with all the handicaps of communication that I have underlined, is such that it makes people sit up and take notice.

It may be said in summary that participation in conferences yielded limited success. What success was attained came in favorable situations and most frequently with some sort of assistance from co-workers. Finally, to function at all in a conference, a deaf person must exert a little more than the usual effort before, during and after the meeting.

The thirty-six respondents who said they did not take part in conferences were asked whether other people in their work groups did so. Nine respondents said that none in their groups attended conferences; five did not reply and one did not know. Of the remaining twenty-one, ten said their exclusion was because of their deafness; nine said they were not required (by their work) to attend; two looked upon conferences as a waste of time.

Other Communication Problems

One of the less obvious communication problems confronting a deaf person is how much news he can obtain through the office grapevine. The value attributed to this source of informal news varied among the respondents. When they were asked whether the information was useful in their work, forty-four (about half of them) said it had little or no value; twenty-eight (about a third) attributed some value; five thought it of great value; ten did not reply.*

Reactions varied from "I never listen to that. It is not useful. It's silly" to "I find that information by the grapevine is very important, both within our organization and also on a much larger scale in the industry."

A colleague spoke of one respondent who was pushing very hard for an appropriation for research in his field:

> The fundamental principles, the daily tasks and the bare bones of what he had to do were communicated to him. Albeit it was in a friendly fashion and a very constructive fashion, yet . . . scuttlebutt and the fringes of politics, the difficulty of getting the appropriation, the competition for the appropriation and so on; he had no feeling for that.

Probably the foregoing attitudes were influenced by the nature of the work done by the respondents. The remark about the grapevine being "silly" was amplified by:

> I don't mix with the people here much lately because I'm paying attention to my experimental work most of the time.

The remark, emphasizing the importance of the grapevine was also elaborated:

Great value was expressed by voluntary praise or superlatives about value of grapevine; *some value* by a plain "yes," "it has value" or other neutral statement; *little value* by a qualified "yes" or "oh, some," "a little."

It's quite necessary that I know of some malfunctioning in the team-work in my organization and I must not allow some one person to be a misfit, so I try to keep abreast of intergroup relationships. My research work is dependent upon grapevine news from the outside. It is important to know what other companies are doing, so I do as much grapevine discussion at conventions as I can.

Others spoke of morale, interpersonal relations, the need to know reactions to projects being pushed. Very probably the extent of dealing with people was a determinant of the interest in the grapevine.

Table 55 shows that fifty-seven (66 per cent) of the eighty-seven respondents felt that they were receiving as much or practically as much information via the grapevine as anyone else, whereas about one-third of the respondents assumed that they received less than did their co-workers.

TABLE 55

AMOUNT OF INFORMATION RECEIVED THROUGH THE GRAPEVINE

Amount of Information	Number	Per Cent
Received as much as anyone else in the department	19	22
Received almost as much as anyone else	38	44
Informed about matters affecting themselves or their work	7	8
Received very little	18	21
Were never informed	5	6
Total	87	101

Questions arise as to why some deaf workers received less of such news than others? Was it due to communication problems *per se* or the degree of gregariousness of the respondent or what? As previously mentioned, attitudes as to value of the grapevine probably affected the interest that the respondents took in it and this evaluation may have arisen from the nature of the respondents' work. One colleague said, "If he's a mixer, his hearing handicap doesn't bother him" in picking up such information. Table 56 indicates that this may be correct, for of those who felt that they received practically as much, or more than, their associates over the grapevine, 63 per cent associated, off the job, frequently with people who hear and only 32 per cent associated less frequently, whereas of those who felt they received less information than co-workers, 40 per cent associated frequently with those who hear and 40 per cent associated less frequently.

TABLE 56

AMOUNT OF INFORMATION RECEIVED THROUGH THE GRAPEVINE,
BY FREQUENCY OF ASSOCIATION WITH PEOPLE WHO HEAR

Frequency of Association	Amount of Information	
	As Much as Others (Per Cent)	Less Than Others (Per Cent)
Frequent	63	40
Average	5	20
Less frequent	32	40
Total	100	100

Speech skills also were factors in participation in the grapevine. Among the fifty-seven respondents who participated as much as, or more than co-workers in grapevine activity, about three-fourths could speak and read lips relatively well. Of the thirty respondents who participated less than did co-workers, the proportion who could speak and read lips with similar ease was closer to one-half.

A question also arises as to how a deaf man secures such information. Since it requires an effort to write or to speak clearly for lip-reading, it might be thought that co-workers who could hear would shrug off the effort to convey such collateral information to a deaf person. From that situation it might follow that a deaf person must *ask* for his grapevine information. Replies of the respondents were quite the opposite of the hypotheses given above; seventy-three (84 per cent) of them were told voluntarily or in social talk at the lunch table, in the car pool or the like. Only nine of the eighty-seven respondents said that they asked directly for such information. It would seem that casual social communication was fairly free and frequent for these deaf workers.

Another difficulty in communication is encountered in dealing with strangers. Colleagues were asked how well the respondents met strangers as compared to other people at their levels of work. As may be seen in Table 57, 63 per cent of the colleagues said that the respondents met strangers as well as or better than other people similarly employed, whereas only 25 per cent rated the respondents as doing less well in this regard. Possibly the respondents were more than ordinarily outgoing or had developed a high tolerance for the possible embarrassments arising from association with people who hear. Also there may have been some exaggeration from a natural desire among the colleagues to give their co-worker a boost during the interview.

Both respondents and colleagues were asked to mention other difficulties which might have hindered the respondents in their work. These were categorized and compared in Table 57.

The categories represented such factors as the following:

1. Communication problems: public speaking, assimilation of others' work activities, reluctance of others to approach a deaf person.
2. Human relations: social and business interaction, supervision, customer contacts.
3. Inefficiency: needing written instructions, missing grapevine information, mispronouncing.
4. Physical risk: fear of damage from overhead cranes, machines and chemical reaction.

Of interest here is the fact that almost twice as many colleagues as respondents said that there were no other difficulties. Also 35 per cent of the respondents cited communication problems, but only 6 per cent of the colleagues did so.

Single-word categories as used in Table 58 tend to obscure the human aspects of these problems. Difficulties perceived by the respondents are illustrated by the following:

> Very often they will come in and ask for me and then say, "Oh, he's deaf? Er, okay, wait a minute, I'll see someone else." Or they can't express themselves through writing so they will talk to other people. . . . I'm very willing to communicate to them to help them with their problems, but they are at a loss.

TABLE 57

MANNER IN WHICH RESPONDENTS MET STRANGERS AS COMPARED BY COLLEAGUES TO THAT OF OTHER BUSINESS ASSOCIATES

Manner of Meeting Strangers	*Number*	*Per Cent*
Better than others	15	17
As well as others	40	46
Comparison not made; colleague laudatory	2	2
Not as well as others	22	25
Respondent not required to meet strangers	2	2
Did not know	3	3
No answer	3	3
Total	87	98

TABLE 58

OTHER DIFFICULTIES IN BUSINESS RELATIONS CAUSED BY
DEAFNESS, AS PERCEIVED BY THE RESPONDENTS
AND THEIR COLLEAGUES

Difficulties	Respondents	Colleagues
Communication	30	5
Human relations	20	13
Inefficiency	1	12
Personality	—	6
Physical risk	—	4
Language	—	2
Other	3*	1†
None	22	40
Did not know	—	1
No answer	11	4
Total	87	—‡

*Laboratory noises by respondent, distraction by deaf visitors, limitations on securing further training.
†Superior forgot respondent was deaf.
‡Column adds to more than the number of respondents because of multiple answers by colleagues.

If I were to, say, go out to lunch with my boss and others . . . or maybe happen to sit next to the chairman of the board . . . well, the conversation will probably be restricted and stilted. . . . Well, you tell yourself anyway that if you were normal, you could have carried on a brilliant conversation that would have earned you a promotion quite fast. I'm jesting, but there is that aspect of the thing.

It is very difficult to make a person feel at ease when he's meeting me. So many people just don't know what deafness really is.

I cannot claim that I get all that I'd like to obtain from the contacts at those (professional) meetings.

Colleagues found other problems:

Different problems arise in the office where we more or less are having an open discussion, even myself not realizing that he can't hear us, we make certain decisions . . . and he won't hear it and consequently he might not realize at a later date that I've made a decision to handle a problem in a certain way simply because I myself made the mistake of forgetting to tell him.

I think that where he has to be alone in, say, policy making—at a policy making level—I think he would suffer. . . . He wouldn't be able to catch the inflections that transpire.

Somebody has to relay it to him and when anybody relays a conversation, he will want to leave out a great deal of details. These may be important and sometimes Respondent, I find, has misunderstood what is going on.

Respondents and colleagues were asked whether deafness might have been of help in the respondent's business affairs. The replies are compared in Table 59:

TABLE 59

WAYS IN WHICH DEAFNESS MIGHT BE HELPFUL AT WORK, AS PERCEIVED BY RESPONDENTS AND COLLEAGUES

Helpfulness	Respondents	Colleagues
Aids concentration	41	65
Overcompensation	5	10
Lessens interpersonal friction	5	2
Lessens undesirable socializing	—	3
Other	3*	1†
Not a help	19	10
Did not know	1	1
No answer	13	5
Total	87	87

*Better opportunities, more patience, verbal agreements by telephone were witnessed.
†Novelty of deafness created favorable attention.

Almost 50 per cent of the respondents and almost 75 per cent of the colleagues referred to deafness as serving to minimize noise disturbance and thus aid concentration. The reference was not wholehearted, however; one respondent put it thus;

> They claim I'm lucky that I can't hear the typewriter, but I think that's a very cheap reason. . . . I could concentrate on my work whether I could hear or whether I was deaf.

A number of colleague qualified their replies in the same direction:

> He can just concentrate on his work. So in that instance it's an asset if you can call being deaf an asset.

> Certainly one could infer that, without outside distraction, one would tend to concentrate better. I hate to put much emphasis on that, however. Again, communication is so much more critical.

Lessening interpersonal friction was illustrated by a colleague:

> Because of his deafness there's less tendency for arguments. . . . It's got to be done in black and white and it's got to be fact; if it's not fact, he just doesn't buy it.

Overcompensation was described by a respondent thus:

> A physical handicap often leads to a stronger character. . . . They turn every effort to their respective jobs.

A rough measure of the feelings of respondents and colleagues about deafness being helpful is shown in Table 60 where the attitude of each respondent is compared to that of his colleague.

In instances were respondent and colleague both expressed opinions, over half agreed that deafness could be helpful to some extent. Of those who disagreed, a large majority of the respondents (nineteen) believed deafness not a help.

TABLE 60

COMPARISON OF ATTITUDES OF RESPONDENTS AND
COLLEAGUES ABOUT DEAFNESS AS A HELP

Attitudes	*Number*
Agree; deafness could be a help	37
Disagree; colleagues believed it could be a help, respondent did not	19
Disagree; respondent believed it could be a help, colleague did not	6
Agree; deafness was not a help	2
Did not know	1
No answer (either respondent or colleague)	22
Total	87

JOB-TAILORING

It is not difficult to imagine a deaf person being eminently qualified for a certain position in every way except some aspect of communication. It may be that the job requires the use of the telephone or frequent conferences or much contact work. The deaf person obviously cannot handle these chores, yet his other qualifications may point just as obviously to him as the logical appointee. Management faces a difficult quandary here, as was attested by a colleague who said:

> When the man who was in charge of the lab . . . resigned, I turned it over to Mr. —— (a hearing co-worker of the respondent). Now, neither of them know this, but I could just as well have placed Mr. Respondent in charge. I gave Mr. —— the job because he could use the telephone and had this not been the case, I would have had a difficult decision. . . . Well, Mr. —— is quitting. He . . . well, we just don't know if we are going to replace him or not . . . so the question now comes up: Can I put Mr. Respondent in charge of a job? . . . I think if I had a younger man to help Mr. Respondent, the lab would run smoothly . . . and let Mr. Respondent be in charge of the place because it is in him that I have my talent. . . . I would be interested in your comment if you have any experience with how this kind of a system has worked in the past.

This difficulty occurred in a small research laboratory. In a large concern the problem could be much greater, for jobs there must dovetail in a complex mosaic interjoined by various communication techniques, including importantly the telephone and the conference. Change one of such jobs suddenly and the whole bureaucracy may be jarred. Hence, it is of interest to know if many of the respondents had been advanced to jobs which were of necessity altered—tailored to fit the applicant as it were.

Respondents were asked: "If a job is filled by a deaf man, some things about it may have to be changed because of mechanical difficulties in communication. Was your present job changed in any way to make it fit you better?" Table 61 indicates that a majority of the respondents (62 per cent) did not believe there had been changes made to fit the job to them.

TABLE 61

CHANGES IN JOB FUNCTIONS CAUSED BY DEAFNESS,
AS PERCEIVED BY RESPONDENTS

Changes	*Number*
Changed to accommodate to telephone	19*
Changed to eliminate contacts with the public	4
Changed to accommodate to conferences	3
Changed because of communication with superior	1
No, not changed	54
Did not know	2
No answer	4
Total	87

*One respondent also listed elimination of public contacts.

Of the twenty-seven respondents who did report that job changes were made because of their deafness, nineteen said the changes were made to accommodate to the telephone. Accommodation was accomplished by eliminating the duties or by having a substitute assume them or by arranging for assistance to the respondent in carrying out such duties.

When colleagues were asked the same question, only twelve stated that the respondent's job had been changed to fit him; sixty-one said it had not been changed; three did not know and eleven did not answer. Of the twelve who reported changes, three said that the changes in the respondent's job had affected other jobs.

It would seem that the respondents' careers were not so greatly obstructed by inability to use the telephone or to function in conferences as the respondents imagined or that possibly their colleagues were less conscious of the effects of disabilities such as these.

Yet the deaf professional man's career can be hampered as was witnessed by a colleague:

> When I came here, Mr. Respondent had my job. He was the supervisor. . . . Ours is not routine (work). It's development of methods and performing investigations and things like that. Mr. Respondent had charge of it and he did a very effective job of it from a technical standpoint. Whether it's justified or not, management saw fit to move him out of that job and put me in that job, but only because of the communication limitations of Mr. Respondent. (The respondent was given a new title and certain high-level responsibilities not involving oral communication.)

Nevertheless, the general attitude among colleagues was:

> I think that a person with a little forethought and ingenuity can arrange his (a deaf person's) work assignments, his position, his relative spot in an organization in such a way as to minimize this (communication difficulty) . . . and have him work closely with one or two individuals so that they can establish this ease of communication . . . I'm not saying that you'd be giving something away for nothing because you'd be using his knowledge and his brain.

One respondent said that his department was concerned with sales and research and that he was excused from the sales functions and put on the jobs requiring concentration and freedom from the telephone.

One respondent spoke of a change of attitude on his part:

> For the first ten years I rejected any special assistance, which was a mistake. It was shortsighted because it deprived my program of what special knowledge I had. We should use the special help we need to make our contribution more available, so I have moved in that direction now.

Changes to adapt to a top level job were described by another respondent:

> After it was decided that my responsibility should be increased to include the management of staff activities . . . the board of trustees made adjustments for the manner of holding the meetings. This adjustment involved having one of my immediate associates—either my secretary or one of my two assistant directors—help in handling the meeting. They would read the reports or summarize them orally, then give me the gist of their discussion passed around the table. They would give me that

in writing or notes. The notes were used later in writing minutes of the meeting. But by having someone next to me taking notes, it is possible for me to lead the discussion in the way I want it to be held and the way it should proceed.

A deaf person's advancement may be less a matter of climbing an established career ladder than assuming extra responsibility at a normally lower level position. In other words, it is possible for a person to grow through experience and study to the point where his position grows in stature, responsibility and salary commensurate to his abilities.

A colleague in a research laboratory of a large industrial firm mentioned just such a situation, although it had been administratively formalized and a hierarchy established for staff specialists:

> But we finally convinced him (the respondent), and have proven to him by monetary advances along specialist lines, that he doesn't have to be a supervisor to get ahead. As far as I know, he's perfectly satisfied. He's actually making more money than the fellow who's technically his supervisor.

Another colleague said:

> No, he's changed the job to enlarge it far beyond the scope of what it was when he came in.

LOST OPPORTUNITIES

If colleagues of deaf professional workers were as appreciative of deaf persons' abilities as this research seems to show, why then did *The Survey of Occupational Conditions Among the Deaf* report only 6.6 per cent of its respondents to be in professional positions (and over half of these as teachers in schools for the deaf) in comparison to 10.6 per cent among the general population?[2] Did this imply an inability of deaf persons to meet job requirements or was it due to discrimination? And how do deaf people look upon these lost opportunities?

Present these questions to a group of deaf persons and the replies will be as varied as the experiences of each individual. Some are quick to cry discrimination; others, like Dr. Schowe (p. 64), point to a need for employment officials to consider more than just the technical qualifications for a job.

To tap their experiences in this direction, the respondents in this study were asked, "Has a job, a promotion or a chance to present your ideas ever been denied you because of your deafness?" Free answers were sought, but probes were used to elicit details of what denials occurred, what the respondents did and what the final results were. Actual denials of opportunity were reported by twenty-eight respondents, a little less than a third of the total; fifty-five answered that such denials of opportunity had not occurred to them. No replies were given by two respondents and two said they did not know. However, an awareness that a career ceiling did exist was indicated by twenty-two of the fifty-five who reported no actual denial.

A good many of the denials of opportunity occurred in seeking employment, an area covered in Chapter IV. One respondent was quite specific:

> My rehabilitation counselor phoned and asked for an appointment but —— company said, "No, he will not be hired. He is deaf. We do not hire deaf, blind or any handicapped."

As regards promotions:

> There was a vacancy as assistant director of —— work. I asked for the job. They were quite frank in saying that the position required communication and that has happened more than twice.

> My director is sixty-nine this year; he will be seventy next year, the compulsory retirement age. . . . His successor will be a young man—I say young, he's forty—who was my assistant for most of the ten years he has worked for this outfit. He is a very capable young man; he ought to be, I trained him. The big difference between him and me is that he can hear . . . The board feels that they cannot risk having me as director. . . . He represents the board before interested organizations . . . must make speeches before groups of people outside. . . . They told me they had the greatest respect and admiration for me, but they said I couldn't do that. I asked them why they couldn't do it and have my assistant do the public relations. They said they can't have an assistant director do that. . . . I can't be too critical of them. I appreciate the difficulties they had, but that's the situation.

> The boss gave me a promotion, but the front office objected because of my handicap. . . . I got a promotion many times up until that time. I don't think I'll get any more from here on in. . . . I won't be able to go any higher because higher jobs require supervision and things like that.

> There was a job in another office (of the same concern). . . . After he found out I couldn't hear, he wouldn't even see me. . . .

The job ceiling was noted by a colleague:

> They are excellent in their field. We are fortunate that they are content. . . . They do a very good job. They are very careful and we can hold them, have them much longer than we could have kept the average hearing person in this field.

One factor limiting opportunities for promotion is the difficulty of public contact:

> If it hadn't been for my deafness . . . I could have had that job. . . . However, that entails 80 or 90 per cent public contact—handling people. I just couldn't do that.

A refreshing attitude toward public contacts by a deaf employee was expressed by a colleague:

> I said (to a customer), "All right, I have a man but he is absolutely deaf and dumb . . . if you don't mind a little bit of slow cooperation with this fellow, he'll do a heads up job for you and he'll understand your problem. Everything will work out beautifully for you if you just don't mind being a little patient with lip reading and trying to understand his conversation and maybe you'll have to write a few things." He went out there and did the job hands down and for the estimated price. Later on I called up the outfit and said, "How did he do? Suppose we do this again with someone else?" . . . (They replied) "Fine, as a matter of fact he was sort of a lark. We rather enjoyed the whole business."

A respondent felt left out of conferences:

> I was too busy working to watch the others. Every once in a while they would have a group conference by themselves. They left me out because I wouldn't get anything out of it. But if I had been a part of the group conversation, I am pretty sure I could have contributed quite a few things. I didn't improve my position in that company.

Business pressures resulted in dismissal of one respondent:

> He (the employer) was a very patient man, but under pressure of business it was impossible. . . . He began to become exasperated by the inability to discuss the problems which were coming out at the time, so he had to let me go. . . . As far as technical competence and ability with chemistry (went), there was no problem, but he needed somebody to take over his responsibilities outside.

These experiences bring up the question of what deaf workers ascribe as reasons for opportunities denied. In all but a few instances, the fifty respondents who had experienced, sensed or anticipated denial of opportunity because of deafness attributed it to communication problems. Most of the eleven who cited their inability to do the work qualified the reason by adding something about the telephone or conferences being hindrances to performance. Twenty-seven mentioned incapacity to deal with either co-workers or the public or both. Four respondents cited company policy against hiring deaf persons. Of these fifty respondents, twenty-six recognized the personal incapacity; eleven denied that they were incapable; eight ascribed other reasons and five were unable to answer. The general impression is that a majority of the respondents had experienced or anticipated denial of opportunity due to deafness and that, in the main, they recognized their limitations.

As might be expected, salience of deafness* relates positively to the experience or feeling of denial of opportunity. Of the fifty who experienced or felt denial, thirty-one (62 per cent) were in the higher levels in the salience of deafness index, whereas of those thirty-three who imputed no denial of opportunity, nineteen (58 per cent) were less conscious of their deafness. Whether the experience had caused a stronger awareness of the handicap or whether the handicap had caused or sharpened awareness of the denial was not revealed.

PROFESSIONAL AFFILIATIONS

A professional worker is generally committed to a career rather than a job. He looks to his professional peers for recognition, mutual aid with problems, general advancement of knowledge in his field. Many persons consider membership in professional organizations to be an integral part of a professional career. These organizations function to a large extent through lectures, seminars and conventions where oral communication is a dominant factor. How do deaf people function in this aspect of their professional careers?

Forty-five (52 per cent) of the respondents were members of one professional association or more. The group represented sixty-eight professional organizations. Only a few organizations had more than one member from among the respondents: American Chemical Society, eighteen; American Association for the Advancement of Science,

---

*For a description of an index of this trait, see pp. 128-131 and Appendix E.

four; Sigma Xi, four; New York Academy of Sciences, three; Ogden (Utah) Engineers Club, two; American Statistical Association, two.

There was a relationship between membership in professional groups and speech skills as may be seen in Table 62.

TABLE 62

MEMBERSHIP IN PROFESSIONAL ORGANIZATIONS, BY SPEECH SKILLS

| | Membership | |
| | Members | Nonmembers |
Speech Skills	Per Cent	Per Cent
Expressive—Associates understood:		
Almost everything said	91	58
Occasional word or less	9	42
Total	100	100
Respondents	(45)*	(41)*
Receptive—Respondent understood:		
Short conversation or more	80	44
Simple sentence or less	20	56
Total	100	100
Respondents	(45)*	(41)*

*One respondent gave no answer concerning membership in professional groups.

Of those who were members of professional societies, nine out of ten had adequate speech and eight out of ten could understand through lipreading an ordinary conversation. On the other hand, of those who were not members, 42 per cent used speech only for an occasional word or not at all and 56 per cent could lipread only short, simple sentences or an occasional isolated word. The inference seems to be that speech difficulties inhibit membership in such societies.

Supporting the preceding inference in part is Table 63, which shows that a majority of respondents who were members of professional societies associated frequently with people who hear, whereas

TABLE 63

MEMBERSHIP IN PROFESSIONAL ORGANIZATIONS, BY
FREQUENCY OF ASSOCIATION WITH PEOPLE WHO HEAR

| *Frequency of Association with People Who Hear* | Membership | |
	Members Per Cent	*Nonmembers Per Cent*
Frequently	64	44
Average	16	5
Infrequently	20	51
Total	100	100
Respondents	(45)*	(41)*

*One respondent gave no answer concerning membership in professional groups.

a majority of nonmembers associated infrequently with hearing persons.

Membership in professional organizations also varied with educational level attained. Of the member group, 62 per cent had undertaken study beyond the bachelor's degree, whereas only 27 per cent of the non-members had done so. Specialized training of graduate students and their early commitment to their professions probably were determinants.

Salience of deafness showed an inverse relationship. Of the respondents who were members of professional organizations, 53 per cent had a low salience of deafness, whereas 63 per cent of non-members had a high salience of deafness. Consciousness of the drawbacks of deafness to communication and to easy socializing was probably the underlying factor.

Not all members attended meetings regularly. Only ten of the forty-five organization members said that they attended regularly. Eighteen said sometimes, six rarely, and eleven never. The chief reason given for not attending or for rarely doing so was the inability to follow the proceedings. A few respondents did enjoy the meetings for reasons expressed by one respondent thus: "I learn a lot about what is going on in the field. . . . I think I contribute a lot, too."

Respondents who attended professional meetings were asked what was the value of the meetings to them. Information and new ideas and contacts with their professional peers were the dominant values, thirty-four respondents naming one or more of these. Three cited prestige; one each cited business contacts, publications and socializing and five did not answer.

Of the forty-five respondents who belonged to professional organizations, sixteen had presented papers at such meetings. Two of the sixteen stated that they read these papers themselves; eleven turned the task over to someone else, a colleague or a subordinate; three did not reply. Assistance was required for question periods following the readings; in six cases, the person assisting read the paper and handled the question session. In six other cases, the assistant only relayed the questions to the respondent. One respondent asked that questions be submitted to him in writing.

EFFECTIVENESS ON THE JOB

With all the problems and barriers they faced, most of the respondents were still considered superior workers, according to the colleagues interviewed (Table 64). Only four colleagues said that the respondent, on the whole, handled his job less well than other workers doing similar tasks. Seventy-eight (90 per cent) of the respondents were rated as doing as well as their co-workers and fifty-six of these (64 per cent of all) as doing better than associates on the same job. These opinions were held by colleagues of all ranks in the occupational hierarchy.

Many spontaneous words of praise were elicited by the question about effectiveness at work:

> In his field he's tops as far as I'm concerned.
>
> He's an extremely capable man. He has a wonderful mind.
>
> He's a special individual. I can't find *anyone* even with all their hearing and speech intact who could even approximate his proficiency in his particular area.
>
> I think he overcompensates, so to speak. In other words, he feels that he's behind to start with and he probably works a little harder and gives a little more effort to it and this, coupled with the fact that he has the ability not to be distracted, ends up by making him better than the average. . . . It will get harder as he goes up the scale, I think . . . then the communication problems would multiply. . . .
>
> If we could have more people of his capabilities, I wouldn't care if they were deaf and blind.

Colleagues were asked why, in their opinions, the respondents were relatively successful in their occupations. Their free answers were put in categories of capabilities, attitudes and training, as is shown in Table 65.

In regard to *mental abilities,* colleagues spoke of keenness, memory, analytical talent and so on; *skills* were described as talent, care, competence; *ambition* was expressed as courage, self-confidence, keenness of work, aggressiveness; *compliance* described cooperation and courteous attitudes. Attitude toward the handicap covered jovial acceptance, lack of inferiority feelings, self-reliance.

TABLE 64

EFFECTIVENESS ON THE JOB COMPARED TO CO-WORKERS, AS PERCEIVED BY COLLEAGUES, BY RANK OF COLLEAGUES

Rank of Colleague	Total	Comparison to Co-workers				
		Better	As well	Less well	Declined to Compare	No Answer
Chief executive	8	6	1			1
Vice executive	2	1	1			
Division head	9	7	1	1		
Assistant division head	5	3	1	1		
Department head	14	11	2	1	1	
Professional supervisor	29	16	10	2	1	
Professional staff member	14	9	5			
Group supervisor	1	1				
Clerical worker	3	2			1	
No answer	2		1			1
Total	87	56	22	4	3	2

TABLE 65

REASONS ASCRIBED BY COLLEAGUES FOR
RESPONDENTS' SUCCESS AT WORK

Reasons for Success at Work	Number
Capabilities—Mentality	52
Capabilities—Skill	27
Attitudes—Ambition	32
Attitudes—Compliance	5
Attitudes—Acceptance of handicap	5
Training—Education	6
Training—Experience	5
Training—Education and experience	4
Other	3*
No colleague	1
Total	—†

*Family help, 2; nature of work (engineering), 1.
†Total exceeds 87 because of multiple answers.

SUMMARY

The chief on-the-job problems of these deaf professional workers arose from two managerial tools—the telephone and the group conference. Although considerable ingenuity by respondents and accommodation by co-workers had alleviated these difficulties, still they were recognized as significant handicaps. Another area of difficulty was participation in the organization's grapevine; half of the respondents considered grapevine news of small value. Other difficulties were classified as inefficiency, human relations, personality, physical risk. Generally, colleagues perceived less of difficulties than did respondents and cited more possible areas where deafness might be helpful.

Few respondents were aware of any changes made in their jobs to compensate for their handicaps; most of the changes were made to accommodate to the telephone. Only a third of the respondents cited actual lost opportunities because of their deafness, but over half were aware of a ceiling upon advancement at levels where person-to-person contacts were frequent. Half of the respondents were members of professional organizations and of these only a few attended meetings regularly or had read papers at professional meetings. Despite the difficulties encountered, the performances of 90 per cent of the respondents were rated by colleagues as being as good as or better than those of their co-workers.

Chapter VII

OCCUPATIONAL MOBILITY

Does the American dream of freedom to rise through the strata of society apply to deaf persons? In the words of the social scientists, is the deaf man mobile? Can he climb the occupational ladder?

It would seem that in theory the American dream does apply to deaf persons. The concept of the United States as an open society with a minimum of caste barriers is upheld for deaf people by an elaborate educational system culminating in the only college for such persons in the world. The United States Vocational Rehabilitation Administration and other agencies of the national and state governments expend great efforts to help deaf persons to realize their employment potential. And finally there are deaf persons in high-level employment as professional and managerial officials.

Does mobility create added strains for the deaf person? Or put another way, does deafness increase the difficulty of achieving and maintaining occupational mobility and does it set a limit upon the occupational level which a deaf person may attain?

Occupational mobility can be viewed in three or more frames: intergenerational mobility, mobility in the labor market and mobility—vertical and horizontal—within the firm.

It is occupational mobility in these three aspects that is considered in relation to the respondents. How did they move in relation to the occupational strata of their fathers? Did they change jobs often and why? Did they rise within their firms?

INTERGENERATIONAL MOBILITY

As regards intergenerational mobility, it may be seen from Table 66 that a large proportion (58 per cent) of the fathers of the respondents came from the higher occupational levels of professionals and managers, levels similar to those achieved by the respondents

There were eighteen respondents in positions higher on the indus-

TABLE 66
OCCUPATIONS OF RESPONDENTS' FATHERS

Occupation	Number	Per Cent
Professional, technical and kindred workers	28	32
Managers, officials and proprietors (farm)	4	5
Managers, officials and proprietors (non-farm)	18	21
Clerical, sales and kindred workers	4	5
Craftsmen, foremen and kindred workers	25	29
Operatives and kindred workers	3	3
Laborers	1	1
Other	2*	2
Unemployed	1	1
No answer	1	1
Total	87	100

*Fathers died when respondents were small children.

occupational levels higher than those of their fathers, evidence that opportunity does exist for deaf workers.

Intergenerational influences upon occupational aspirations and achievements of young people are complex. Family attitudes, social environment, occupational opportunities, educational aims, all influence the person's values and possibly aid his efforts for training, employment and promotion.

A direct influence was employment in the family business. There were four respondents who were either employed in the family business or had had fathers as direct sponsors.

There were eighteen respondents in positions higher on the industrial hierarchy than that of professional staff persons. Of these eighteen, two had had fathers in blue-collar occupations. Of thirty-seven respondents who earned more than $8,000 a year, twenty-five (over two-thirds) were from families of the white-collar class.

Among the measurable intergenerational influences is the amount of education acquired. A distinct relationship between the occupations of fathers and the highest educational level attained by respondents is revealed in Table 29. Sons of white-collar workers constituted almost 90 per cent of those with graduate degrees, 60 per cent of those with bachelor's degrees and 52 per cent of those who attended but were not graduated from college. In addition, the eighteen (out of thirty) holders of college degrees who came from blue-collar families included fourteen who had attended Gallaudet College, where it was possible to have total financial aid if necessary, a boon to the less well-to-do. All writers on occupational mobility emphasize the value of a college education to the mobile man, especially in the professions, where training must be extensive and commitment early.

On the whole, it can be said that the majority of the respondents were not mobile intergenerationally; that is, a majority of them did not rise to higher occupational strata than their parents had reached. Yet this majority is not so large as to justify a statement that occupational advancement beyond the level achieved by their fathers is closed to deaf workers.

LABOR MARKET MOBILITY

Professional workers have been found by a number of investigations to be relatively stable in occupational mobility and job mobility. As to occupation, professional workers are careerists and as such have committed themselves to a pattern of expectations often extending throughout their working lives. Lipset and Malm[9] found that 78 per cent of the professional people they studied had started as professionals and commented:

> The propensity of many to remain in the occupational category in which they started is related also to the degree of training required for a full-fledged worker. Thus, professional, semi-professional, and skilled workers are less likely to evidence mobility between their first and present jobs than other groups.

Also, as regards a group of occupations as dominated by the sciences as was that of the respondents, Mapheus Smith's[14] comment is pertinent:

> Scientists gain relatively less from change in position and relatively more from evaluation of actual work done. The stronger institutional affiliations of scientists also aid in recognition, so that a scientist resident for a long time in the same situation has far more chance of recognition than a person exhibiting the same degree of stability in another occupation.

Deaf people were found by Bigman[2] to be "very stable on the job." He speculated that the prospect of prejudice in moving into a new job might make the deaf worker "cling to the job he has, whatever it is, more tenaciously than his hearing fellow."

In view of all these factors promoting stability of employment, it was to be expected that the respondents would be an extremely stable group of workers. Based upon Miller and Form's[11] definition of a stable career—three employers or fewer before age thirty-five or 4.6 employers or fewer (four used in this study) during entire work history—it may be said that 76 per cent of respondents were stably employed (Table 67). All respondents below age thirty-five except one had held three jobs or fewer.

TABLE 67

JOB STABILITY: NUMBER OF JOBS HELD, BY AGE

Age	Total	Number of Jobs Held											
		1	2	3	4	5	6	7	8	9	10	11	12
Under 25	1	1											
25-34	20	6	11	2	1								
35-44	25	8	4	5	2	4	1			1			
45-54	27	4	4	5	4	4	2	1	1	1			1
55-64	10	6		1		1			1	1			
65 and over	4			1	1	1	1						
Total	87	25	19	14	8	10	4	1	2	2	1	—	1

That the majority of "unstable" employees were in the age group between forty-five and fifty-four years arouses a suspicion that the instability of some may have been involuntary and due to the distorted economic situation of the 1930's, when persons in this age group entered the labor force. The depression probably caused more early job changes in the search for a professional niche than is usual.

Examination of the individual records of the twenty-one persons who had held five or more jobs during their working lives revealed that their longest period in one job ranged from four to forty years; the mean one-job tenure was 13.6 years. A ratio of longest job tenure to employment was calculated for all employees by dividing the longest period of years in one job by the total number of years at work. This calculation yielded a ratio showing the per cent of the total work life spent in a single job. Of the twenty-one employees classified in unstable careers, twelve had employment tenure ratios above 50 per cent; four above 75 per cent. The mean employment tenure ratio was 53 per cent. It may be ventured, then, that certainly seventy (81 per cent) and possible seventy-eight (90 per cent) of the respondents have had stable employment records in spite of the difficulties experienced by some in settling into their career positions.

Table 68 compares the longest period of employment in one job

TABLE 68

LONGEST PERIOD OF EMPLOYMENT IN ONE JOB*

Longest Period of Employment (Years)	Respondents (Per Cent)	The Survey of Occupational Conditions Among the Deaf Respondents (Per Cent)
Under 1	—	4.1
1 - 2	5	12.2
3 - 5	23	17.9
6 - 10	13	22.5
11 - 20	36	25.6
Over 20	24	16.7
Not reported	—	1.0
Total Respondents	101 (87)	100.0 (8,927)

*Respondents and respondents for *The Survey of Occupational Conditions Among the Deaf* who had been employed during previous ten years.

among the respondents and among 8,927 deaf workers examined in *Occupational Conditions Among the Deaf*.

There was a definite tendency among the present respondents toward longer tenure in one job; 60 per cent of the present respondents had worked in one job for over ten years as compared to 42.3 per cent of the Bigman group. Some biases exist between the two schedules, however: the current respondents were chosen on the basis of permanency of occupation and also were older as a group (median age, forty-four years) than the *Survey of Occupational Conditions* group (37.7 years).

Another measure of stability is the employment tenure ratio, just mentioned, which measures the proportion of each respondent's working life that was spent with one employer. The distribution for all respondents is given in Table 69.

There are clusters at two intervals in the range of the ratio of employment tenure: 40 per cent had spent 90 to 100 per cent of their working lives with one employer and an identical 40 per cent had spent 50 to 70 per cent of their careers with one employer. The median ratio for the group is 73 per cent of working life with one employer. Only 13 per cent of the respondents had spent less than half of their careers at one job; 29 per cent of them had been at only one job in their entire working lives.

In considering why there was high stability of employment among

TABLE 69
RATIO OF EMPLOYMENT TENURE

Ratio of Employment Tenure (Per Cent)	Respondents Number	Per Cent
Under 29	2	2
30 - 39	5	6
40 - 49	4	5
50 - 59	14	16
60 - 69	10	11
70 - 79	11	13
80 - 89	6	7
90 - 99	10	11
100	25	29
Total	87	100

the respondents, it is well to examine their own conceptions about the frequency of their job changes. Respondents were asked, "Compared to other persons in your occupation, do you think you have changed jobs often?" They were then presented a card on which frequency was scaled as "very often," "fairly often," "fairly seldom," and "very seldom." Five respondents added the classification "never." In Table 70, the perceived frequency of change is compared to the actual frequency of change as revealed in their employment histories.

Only eight respondents felt that they had changed their employers often and only one of these thought that the frequency was very often. Sixty-one thought that they had changed jobs very seldom or never, including a respondent who had actually changed jobs twelve times.

The correspondence between the respondents' perception and actual frequency of change is close at the lower end of the scale. Of the sixty-four who had changed jobs three or fewer times, sixty-two thought their frequency of change was seldom or never. However,

TABLE 70
PERCEIVED FREQUENCY OF JOB CHANGES, BY ACTUAL
FREQUENCY OF JOB CHANGES

Perceived Frequency of Changes	Total	None	1	2	3	4	5	6	7	8	9	10	11	12
Very often	1								1					
Fairly often	7		1		1	2	1			1	1			
Fairly seldom	16	2	4	3	3	3	1							
Very seldom	56	16	14	11	4	5	2	1	1	1				1
Never	5	5												
No answer	2	2												
Total	87	25	19	14	8	10	4	1	2	2	1			1

out of the twenty-one who changed four or more times, fifteen judged changes to have been seldom.

The respondents were asked, "In your opinion, why have you moved around so (seldom, often)?" No probing was done to elicit opinions as to the effect of deafness upon the frequency of their job changes, but in analyzing replies, any reference to deafness was coded and counted. Only five of the eighty-seven respondents mentioned deafness as a factor in their employment mobility. Of course, it is probable that deafness may have actually conditioned the reasons they did give for frequency or infrequency of job changes. The reasons cited are shown in Table 71.

TABLE 71

REASONS FOR FREQUENCY AND INFREQUENCY OF JOB CHANGES

Reasons	Number	Per Cent
Frequency of changes:		
Desire to improve	10	11
Desire to improve and interpersonal difficulties	1	1
Health	1	1
Infrequency of changes:		
Satisfied with job and conditions	47	54
Disliked change	9	10
Disliked change and satisfied with job	4	5
Disliked change and limited contacts for job-seeking	2	2
Deafness	5	6
Other reasons	3*	3
No reason	1	1
No answer	4	4
Total	87	100

*Just started in first job, 1; planning to study for more advanced degree, 2.

It might be imagined that skill, or lack of it, in speech and lipreading would affect the willingness to move to a new job. Doubts about his acceptance by prospective co-workers might make him, in Bigman's[2] words, "cling tenaciously to his present job." When perceived frequency of job changes was examined in relation to speech skills (Table 72), there was no particular variation evident except that those with the least skill in speech and lipreading thought that they had changed jobs often. Similar proportions occurred when means of communication used by respondents were analyzed in the same way. Certain classifications not readily categorized are eliminated from this table.

Frequency of association with people who hear also distributed

TABLE 72
FREQUENCY OF JOB CHANGES, BY SPEECH SKILLS, AS PERCEIVED BY RESPONDENTS

Speech Skills	Total		Perceived Frequency of Job Changes				
			Very Often	Fairly Often	Fairly Seldom	Very Seldom	Never
	Number	Per Cent	Per Cent	Per Cent	Per Cent	Per Cent	Per Cent
Expressive							
Associates understood:							
Practically all said	36	100	3	6	19	58	14
Almost everything said	28	101		4	18	79	
Occasional word or two	18	100		22	17	61	
Total	82	100	1	9	18	66	6
Receptive							
Respondents understood:							
Almost everything said	18	100		6	33	44	17
Short conversation	36	100		8	14	72	6
Short, simple sentences	18	101		6	17	78	
Occasional word	11	100	9	18	18	55	
Total	83	99	1	8	19	65	6

evenly for the various categories of changing jobs. Excluding the vagaries of small numbers, the proportions of perceived frequencies of job changes are remarkably alike in Table 73.

Comments of respondents which were categorized as "satisfied with job and conditions" included such as: "I have a very keen interest in my work"; "We have a very liberal retirement plan, sick leave, a generous life insurance program"; "I've always had a high regard for . . . the men I work with"; "I found my niche"; "At first I moved around a little. . . . I'm satisfied now"; "I think it important to have

TABLE 73
FREQUENCY OF JOB CHANGES, BY FREQUENCY OF ASSOCIATION WITH PEOPLE WHO HEAR, AS PERCEIVED BY RESPONDENTS

Perceived Frequency of Job Changes	Frequency of Association With People Who Hear				
	Very Frequent	Frequent	Average	Less Frequent	Rare
	Per Cent	Per Cent	Per Cent	Per Cent	Per Cent
Often	11	10	11	7	
Seldom or never	83	90	89	89	100
No answer	6			4	
Total (per cent)	100	100	100	100	100
(Respondents)	(18)	(30)	(9)	(27)	(3)

firm roots in my own community so that the children will develop a sense of security"; "I like the deaf people in this town."

Those whose responses were classified as disliking change chiefly reacted in aversion to being a job-hopper. One said that there would be a difficult adjustment period for a deaf person fitting into a new group.

Desire to improve generally took the form of broadening of knowledge through varied experience.

Deafness as a bar to frequent job changing was expressed by a few respondents as: "Other employers do not want deaf workers"; "Deafness prevents me from taking part in conferences"; "Employers do not understand the deaf"; "The deaf know when they have a good thing."

What had been the results of the stable careers of these respondents? Had they been held back by lack of mobility or had recognition come to them in part from their institutional affiliation, as was suggested regarding scientists by Mapheus Smith?

As regards earnings, Table 74 shows very little variation among the salary levels between the mobile men and those who did not change jobs. Among respondents with salaries over $10,000, however, ten of the eleven respondents were infrequent job changers.

TABLE 74
ACTUAL FREQUENCY OF JOB CHANGES, BY PRESENT INCOME

Frequency of Job Changes	Total	Present Income	
		Under $8,000	Over $8,000
Three or less	76	74	74
More than three	24	26	26
Total	100	100	100

Another measure of gain from mobility or from stability is the respondent's position in the firm's organizational hierarchy. Of nineteen respondents who had positions higher than professional staff, three had changed jobs more than three times.

It is evident that these deaf professional workers fared better, as a rule, when they stayed with their employers.

MOBILITY WITHIN THE FIRM

Two measures of vertical mobility exist for the respondents: direction of income changes and employment level attained.

An assessment of each respondent's work history revealed his average income from each job (with a new employer). It was also noted whether the respondent's income rose steadily, fluctuated or remained level during his working career. Table 75 shows a steadily rising income for almost all (90 per cent) of the respondents.

TABLE 75

DIRECTION OF INCOME CHANGES DURING
RESPONDENTS' WORKING LIVES

Direction of Income Changes	Number	Per Cent
Rising steadily	78	90
Fluctuating	7	8
Level	1	1
No answer	1	1
Total	87	100

Most of the respondents (sixty-six of them) were members of the professional staff of their firms. This title may describe the person whose rank compares to the third level of administration in a giant corporation's research laboratory, or a routine analytical chemist in a small independent laboratory or a draftsman in a large force. The nineteen respondents who were ranked higher than professional staff had administrative responsibilities large or small; here again the weight of the position varied with the size of the concern.

To rise in any hierarchy is supposed to require long service and familiarity with the needs and resources of the firm. Table 76 indicates that all but two of the nineteen respondents with administrative responsibilities had served ten or more years with one firm.

Of the twenty-four respondents who had served twenty years or more in one job, twelve had been given administrative responsibilities. Of the three respondents ranked as chief executives, one was the head of a research laboratory and two were partners in their own small firms.

While length of service is a factor in promotion to administrative posts, devotion to a single employer does not necessarily always bring the same results. As shown in Table 77, all of the administrators had been with their firms half of their working lives or longer. Almost 85 per cent of the staff people had been with their firms just as long. Over a fourth of the staff people had been with their present employer all their working lives. Of course, other variables, such as the

TABLE 76
LEVEL OF EMPLOYMENT ATTAINED, BY LONGEST
PERIOD OF YEARS WITH ONE EMPLOYER

Level of Employment Attained	Total	Longest Period of Years With One Employer								
		1-4	5-9	10-14	15-19	20-24	25-29	30-34	35-39	40+
Administrator	19	1	1	2	3	6	3		1	2
Professional staff	66	17	12	10	15	6	2	4		
No answer	2		2							
Total	87	18	15	12	18	12	5	4	1	2

TABLE 77

LEVEL OF EMPLOYMENT ATTAINED,
BY RATIO OF EMPLOYMENT TENURE

Level of Employment Attained	Total	Ratio of Employment Tenure					
		Under 50%	*50-69%*	*70-89%*	*90-99%*	*100%*	*No Answer*
Administrators	19		5	3	4	7	
Staff persons	66	11	19	13	5	18	2
No answer							
Total	87	11	24	16	9	25	2

individual's interest in and aptitude for administration, play a larger part than company loyalty.

Are speech skills related to promotion for deaf persons into administrative positions? Speech seemed helpful, for colleagues were able to understand practically all that was said by sixteen of the nineteen respondents who held administrative jobs. Almost everything said by the remaining three was understandable if one listened carefully. The division was less emphatic as regards ability to read the lips. Of the nineteen, six could understand almost everything said; eight, short conversations spoken carefully; four, short simple sentences spoken very carefully; one, an occasional word or two.

Association off the job with people who could hear did not seem to be a consistently deciding factor in selection to administrative positions although there was a tendency toward some frequent association. The administrators associated with hearing people as follows: five very frequently, eight frequently, one average, three less frequently, and two rarely.

Age of occurrence of deafness among the administrators tended toward the later age levels. More than half of these respondents had lost their hearing at age six or after; eight of them after age twelve. Yet eight had become deaf before age six; three of them were born so.

TABLE 78

AGE OF OCCURRENCE OF DEAFNESS:
RESPONDENTS IN ADMINISTRATIVE POSITIONS

Age of Occurrence of Deafness	Number
Born deaf	3
Below age 1	2
3-5	3
6-11	3
12-14	4
15 and over	4
Total	19

Investigation of horizontal mobility in the form of transfer from one department of a firm to another was not made. It was felt that this form of mobility is more peculiar to line officials than to staff workers. The specialist sticks to his last, as a rule.

However, a related aspect of group work was covered in the

question to colleagues, "Is Mr. (Respondent) sometimes assigned to a special job or to do the work of a person who is on vacation or sick leave?" Table 79 indicates that a little over 40 per cent of the respondents were so transferred.

TABLE 79
TRANSFERS TO OTHER JOBS

	Number
Transferred	37
Not transferred	19
Not done here, or not applicable to respondent's type of job	15
Did not know	3
No answer	13
Total	87

Regarding the thirty-four not transferred, fifteen colleagues volunteered that such transfers were not done or were a waste of the respondent's special skills; probably in a good many of the nineteen other cases of respondents not transferred, they would have answered likewise if probed in that direction. In the nineteen cases where "No" was the reply, colleagues were asked whether hearing co-workers were transferred though the respondent was not; ten replied in the affirmative. Transfer to other jobs within the department did not seem to have created difficult problems on the whole. Less than half of the respondents were transferred and a great majority of these did as well as or better than co-workers. For those who were not transferred, the main reason was the specialized nature of the work they did, not difficulties caused by their deafness.

SUMMARY

It may be said that these deaf respondents were, like other professional and scientific workers, very stable on the job. More than three-fourths of them had held fewer than three jobs during their careers and the proportions would have been larger if depression-affected respondents had been eliminated. Job stability did not seem, however, to have greatly affected the incomes or level of employment.

Chapter VIII

ATTITUDES OF AND ABOUT ADULT DEAF PERSONS

A PROPER STUDY of attitudes of deaf persons or of normal persons toward deaf adults would require a separate and quite precise research approach, since attitudes are peculiarly difficult to assess and quantify. Considerable study and careful concept formulation would be a necessary preliminary, too, for there is little or no research literature on attitudes of and about deaf adults. Nevertheless, an inquiry into the occupational adjustment of deaf people cannot disregard attitudes, since they are integral parts of interpersonal relationships. Hence, a few questions were asked about attitudes, associations and interests of respondents and their colleagues, and this chapter offers from them some tentative clues for further study.

Observed general attitudes about deafness are not classified here. To list them would only tend to confuse, for so many of such attitudes—held by the general public and by deaf persons, too—are pure prejudice. These types of misinformation run from the question, "Do they teach braille in your school for the deaf?" to unreasoning suspicions and fears which occur among some deaf persons.

The examination of attitudes here is mainly from the viewpoint of the respondents. Only in discussing relations with co-workers are the views and attitudes of colleagues brought in.

ATTITUDES TOWARD DEAFNESS

Salience of Deafness

Deafness is never an absolute handicap. In the amount of hearing loss itself there is great variation. The effect of deafness on personality is always relative, even in a group homogeneous as to the extent and time of hearing loss. There is no valid stereotype, "the deaf." It can never rationally be said, "This person is deaf, consequently he has this or that personality trait, mental capacity or attitude."

[128]

Instead, it is probable that deafness tends to accentuate character traits or latencies present in the person by nature or by nurture. Thus the person who is by nature aggressive may be made more so by the frustration of communication blocks. Or a person with a tendency to withdraw may find protection from the aches and pains of being deaf by retiring further into his shell. A teen-age hearing loss can cause an emotional storm which wreaks havoc upon the person's life for a number of years to come or, in another person, it can have an almost immediate maturing effect.

The extent of the effect upon native traits may be the most basic aspect of the handicap of deafness. The measurement of this effect, however, is no simple matter. One cannot just approach a deaf person and ask, "How much does deafness affect your thoughts and deeds?" The only result would be a morass of clichés, subjective guesses and noncomparable measures. Nor is there any standardized test to measure this effect and it is doubtful if one could be devised. Yet some inkling of how much a person's handicap pervades his thoughts can be of value in assessing his reactions to life situations.

In this study, a rough index of salience of deafness was used. As is described more fully in Appendix E, the index was constructed by examining seven questions which evoked free answers from the respondents. If a respondent's reply mentioned deafness in any way at all, this question was scored as indicating that the respondent's thought concerning that topic was affected by the awareness that he was deaf. Likewise, it was assumed that the more frequently this awareness was manifested, the higher would be his salience of deafness. The scores were scaled from zero to seven, zero representing the lowest salience of deafness and seven the highest. As may be seen from Table 80, the modal point for the respondents was 2, that these twenty-three respondents mentioned deafness only twice in their answers to seven questions for which they were not cued and to which a reference to deafness was not actually required.

A high salience of deafness (index numbers 6 and 7, for example) was held by only 11 per cent of the respondents. At the lower half of the scale (index number 3 and below) were 65 per cent of the respondents. It may be ventured that as a group these deaf people did not frequently dwell upon their handicap.

TABLE 80
INDEX OF SALIENCE OF DEAFNESS

Index of Salience of Deafness	Number of Respondents	Per Cent
0	3	3
1	9	10
2	23	26
3	22	25
4	9	10
5	11	13
6	9	10
7	1	1
Total	87	98

There is no intention here to make any sort of value judgment regarding the extent of salience of deafness in any individual or group. Awareness of one's handicap can be constructive or destructive. For example, a person may take deafness into consideration frequently to help make realistic plans or to accommodate himself to a situation where he and his handicap are anomalous. Or on the other hand, a deaf person may be in a constant state of self-pity.

There are two possible assumptions regarding salience of deafness as related to frequency of association with people who hear. On the one hand, the deaf person associating more frequently with people who can hear may be less aware of his deafness because the mores and the thinking habits of his associates do not emphasize this handicap. On the other hand, the deaf person's handicap may be brought more forcibly to his attention by contrast with associates who are not so handicapped. The figures in Table 81 bear out the hypothesis of relation between association with people who hear and a low salience of deafness, but the indications are not strongly positive. If index numbers 0-3 are assumed to indicate low salience of deafness and 4-7 high, then of the forty-eight respondents who associated frequently with people who could hear, 75 per cent had a low salience of deafness. For the thirty respondents who associated less frequently with people who could hear, the division was half and half. Possibly the association was less influenced by deafness than by other personality traits.

There was slight indication of a relationship between low salience of deafness and early occurrence of the handicap. Of the fifty-six

TABLE 81

SALIENCE OF DEAFNESS, BY FREQUENCY OF
ASSOCIATION WITH PEOPLE WHO HEAR

Index of Salience of Deafness	Total	Frequency of Association With People Who Hear				
		Very Frequent	Frequent	Average	Less Frequent	Rare
0	3		2	1		
1	9	2	3	2	1	1
2	23	4	11		8	
3	22	4	10	3	4	1
4	9	1	3		5	
5	11	4		2	4	1
6	9	3	1	1	4	
7	1				1	
Total	87	18	30	9	27	3

persons with low salience of deafness, thirty-six (64 per cent) had become deaf before age six, whereas of the thirty with high salience of deafness, fourteen (47 per cent) had become deaf before age six. The relationship here was hardly clear enough to justify exploring causes. Possibly those deafened later in youth were more deeply affected and tended to struggle, consciously or not, to maintain the habits acquired when they could hear and hence they were more aware of their lack of ability to do so.

There was a similar relationship between low salience of deafness and attendance at schools for the deaf. Of the fifty-six respondents who attended schools for the deaf the longest during their elementary and secondary education, forty-one (73 per cent) had a low salience of deafness, whereas 52 per cent of the thirty-one respondents who attended public schools the longest had low salience of deafness. The proportions were quite similar to those for age of occurrence of deafness and, indeed, one might have been the result of the other because respondents deafened early tended to spend the greater part of their educational years in schools for the deaf. Perhaps their long attendance at a school familiar with the handicap and their observance there of many other persons similarly handicapped made their deafness loom less large in their thinking than it would have if they had been the only deaf person in a "normal" group.

Salience of deafness is examined in relation to other elements of the respondents' lives in the sections of this report dealing with those elements.

Levels of Life Satisfaction

A measure of a person's general outlook is the degree of satisfaction with which he looks upon his life and achievements. Each respondent was asked to estimate his or her position on a scale of 10 representing the worst (1) and the best (10) way of life for a person like himself, as he was when interviewed and as he imagined he might be if he could hear. (The best and worst ways of life were the respondents' own concepts; interviewers gave absolutely no cues or assistance for the replies to these questions.) The estimates are shown in Table 82.

TABLE 82

PRESENT LEVEL OF LIFE SATISFACTION* AND
LEVEL ANTICIPATED IF RESPONDENT COULD HEAR

Level of Life Satisfaction	As at Present	If Could Hear
Step 1	1	1
2	—	1
3	2	—
4	2	2
5	7	1
6	15	5
7	14	3
8	13	11
9	9	15
10	12	20
Over 10	—	14
No answer	—	2
Total	75	75

*The questions concerning life satisfaction were rephrased after the pretest; twelve respondents who constituted the pretest group were excluded from this and other tables dealing with the subject.

It can readily be seen that the group anticipated a higher level of satisfaction if they had been able to hear. The median for the actual levels estimated at the time of the interview was 6.79. The median anticipated if the respondents could hear was 8.87. Fourteen respondents were so optimistic over the prospects if they could hear that they said they would be over the top of the scale.

Not all of the respondents felt that they would be higher on the scale of life satisfaction if they could hear. Of the seventy-five queried, fifty-four stated they would be higher if they could hear; thirteen said there would be no difference and six anticipated they would be lower if they could hear. Of the fifty-four who anticipated a higher step, twenty-three thought they would be one step higher; eight, two steps and fifteen, four steps or more.

A question arises as to what this anticipation means. Is it an indication in reverse of a sense of deprivation among the respondents? From their status in life, their own interviews and the opinions of their colleagues, it does not seem likely that the majority of these deaf men and women spent much of their time worrying about their losses because of the handicap. Indeed, a few of the respondents reacted to the question about their status if they could hear with, "I never thought of that." It is more likely that the estimates of a higher position on the scale if they had the advantage of hearing were realistic views of a moderately successful career and reasonably optimistic views of their potential had the handicap been removed.

Each respondent was asked why he would rate a hearing person in just the same situation as he himself as occupying a step higher, lower or the same as that on which he had previously put himself. The replies are categorized in Table 83.

Most of the thirty-eight respondents who related their position on

TABLE 83

REASONS FOR RATINGS ON SCALE OF LIFE SATISFACTION

Reasons	Number
Better level if could hear, because respondent:	(59)*
Could have a better job (be able to put self over, better earnings, more congenial work)	38
Could socialize better (marry, attend meetings, etc.)	18
Would experience less limitations and frustrations, (sell ideas and skills, communicate, avoid prejudices)	13
Could learn more	11
Could enjoy activities requiring hearing (music, lectures, plays, etc.)	10
Could have broader experience	6
Could be of aid to other deaf people	1
No difference anticipated, because respondent:	(10)
Feels deafness not a factor	3
Feels situation would be entirely different if could hear	3
Had overcompensated because of deafness	2
Prefers a quiet life	1
Feels life satisfaction is not affected by occupational status and material things	1
Better level if deaf, because respondent:	
Matured faster because of handicap	1
No answer	5
Total respondents	(75)*

*Total exceeds number of respondents because of multiple answers.

the scale to their jobs felt that if they could hear, they would make better use of the telephone and conferences and deal better with people:

> I could use the telephone. I could probably tell the boss my ideas better by talking to him.
>
> I would have a more penetrating analysis of the problems raised. I would have a more direct approach to a solution rather than get it second-hand.
>
> I could get along on my own better. I wouldn't have to depend on other people for phoning or talking. I could approach more people.
>
> I could talk my way higher. I could handle other men.
>
> I notice there are more opportunities for hearing people . . . well, like in clubs, Rotary, Kiwanis. . . .

Some anticipated a broader world:

> I would be in a larger world if I could hear.
>
> I would have had a more normal upbringing and social life.
>
> A wider, more interesting circle of friends. I have made friends, a broad, cultural world, but it's hard to keep in touch with them when you're deaf.
>
> Because they can use the telephone, they can hear, listen to music, listen to lectures, speak in groups, which I miss a great deal.

Some looked for release from frustrations:

> There is no question in my mind that every deaf person who has any ability . . . is fundamentally a frustrated person. Frustrated because they are constantly comparing themselves, what they are at present, to what they feel they could be if they were not so handicapped. . . . Any deaf person who can achieve any success at all with his handicap could do a great deal better without.

One respondent, though frustrated, recognized the possibility of advance through overcompensation:

> Because I wouldn't be frustrated, that's all. But I wouldn't say it's higher. My neighbor next door. She can hear, has a lovely voice. What a shame—secretary to an electronic engineer. Nice, but she has not used her abilities. . . . I am way, way ahead of her.

The concept of overcompensation was the basis of a "no difference" reply in two instances and was referred to in other context by several:

I don't have a good basis for judging but my high school and earlier schooling prior to deafness did not show any signs of outstanding qualities. I may have tried a little harder to compete after I lost my hearing.

I think that people reach the level that they would have regardless of any handicap. I think I put forth more effort because I have the handicap. . . .

One attributed his "no difference" in level to the nature of his work:

It's because I think the work has been based mostly on ability, engineering know-how or application of yourself to the job rather than one's ability to carry on a conversation with those around him.

One respondent balanced out occupational and other aspects of life:

If I had not lost my hearing, I might have been much more caught up in the whirl of things to the point that I might not have the correct sense of values . . . I might put too much emphasis on the getting ahead and the job itself and might not actually have turned my thoughts to the extracurricular work, so that I might have been farther ahead professionally, but not as far ahead as a man.

One recognized occupational blocks but said:

I have peace of mind—quiet. I think if I could hear, I'd be lost (due to noise, distraction).

The attitude of those unable to answer was expressed this way:

I don't know the answer. I never thought how to answer that question. . . . If I could hear, my thoughts on life would be much changed, I think . . . I never dreamed that I could be able to hear.

If I could hear, I might be a different person. I might have different tastes and things like that.

ATTITUDES TOWARD WORK SITUATION

General Orientation to Work

Dubin[5] classifies workers in three groups as regards their central life interests. *The work-oriented individual's* life centers on his job; his ideals and motivations are related to the institution which employs him. *The community-oriented person's* life centers upon some interest outside the work situation, such as a hobby, civic work, his family;

to such a person, work is a necessity to earn the money needed to follow the pursuit that interests him. *The indifferent person* has shallow and temporary interests and, as yet, no area of involvement or motivation. Obviously the respondents did not fit in this latter group.

The respondents seemed to have been inclined toward the work-oriented pattern. When asked to describe their self-conception of the best way of life, thirty-four of the seventy-five respondents were concerned, in their aspirations, with their work situation, as is shown in Table 84. Also aspirations as to personal character emphasized self improvement (sixteen) and acceptance by others (thirteen), both of which are aspects of a congenial work situation. Community orientation was expressed, however, by concern for family members (thirty-three times) and desire to be of public service (twenty-two times). These aspirations were formulated entirely by the respondents; interviewers had been instructed to avoid direction or assistance with the questions.

Additional evidence of devotion to the job was indicated by colleagues' estimates of respondents' effectiveness on the job. As is shown in Chapter VI, seventy-eight of the eighty-seven respondents were rated as good as or better than their co-workers. In thirty-two instances, this superiority was ascribed to the respondent's ambition and keenness for the work.

Relations with Co-Workers—General

One of the qualities sought in recruiting employees is the ability to get along with co-workers. It would seem that the problem of getting along should be more difficult for a deaf person, since interpersonal relations depend on communication. Social chitchat and the daily exchange of pleasantries would seem to be considerably inhibited by communication difficulties.

Yet when colleagues were asked, "On the whole, have attitudes of people here been favorable to the idea of employing a deaf person like (the respondent)?" seventy of the eighty-six queried said attitudes were favorable. Only three recorded unfavorable attitudes which were colored by elements other than deafness (Table 85). Of course, these answers must be weighed because of the natural tendency to

TABLE 84
ASPIRATIONS OF RESPONDENTS

Aspirations	Number
Personal character:	(35)*
Peace of mind, etc.	1
Be a normal, decent person, etc.	4
Sense of purpose—have a goal or direction in life	2
Self-improvement	16
Acceptance by others	13
Achieve sense of personal worth	5
Resolution of own religious problem	2
Economic situation:	(22)*
Improvement of present standard of living	1
Decent standard of living; enough money; free from debt, worry	6
Preservation of standard of living for self or family	1
Have own business or farm; be able to expand	1
Have own home or land, apartment, or get a better one	11
Have modern conveniences	2
Have wealth to do as wish	3
Job or work situation:	(34)*
Congenial work, pleasant situation, chance for advancement	26
Employment, steady work	3
Success—be adequate in job; contribute to field of work	4
Perform outstanding work—make an important contribution	4
Concern for family members:	(33)
Family life (happy); have children, etc.	31
Children—adequate opportunities	1
Congenial work for family member(s)	1
Religion, morality, public service:	(24)*
Spiritual, ethical or moral revival; less complacency	3
Wants to be useful to others	22
Deafness:	(10)*
Associate with hearing people	9
Help the deaf	7
Associate with deaf people	7
Be like hearing people	4
Enjoy activities requiring ability to hear	4
Excel hearing people	1
Accept handicap positively	1
Refuse to bow to handicap	1
General:	(10)*
Maintain status quo	6
Adequate social life and contacts	2
No hopes or aspirations	1
Live enjoyably	1
Do the best you can with what you have	1
Live in a small town	1
Miscellaneous:	(29)*
Recreation and leisure	25
Personal freedom of speech, movement, etc.	6
Total respondents	75

*Totals exceed numbers of respondents because of multiple answers.

TABLE 85

ATTITUDES OF CO-WORKERS TOWARD DEAF WORKERS,
AS PERCEIVED BY COLLEAGUES

Attitudes	Number
Strongly favorable	36
Favorable	34
Neutral	7
Unfavorable	3
Did not know	3
No answer	3
Total	86*

*No colleague interview was available for one respondent.

want to put the best foot forward for a fellow worker, but the good opinions expressed are nonetheless impressive.

Colleagues were impressed with some of the respondents' attitudes toward the handicap:

> It is sometimes surprising to me, certainly when I first came here, to see how completely his handicap is overlooked. . . . A jocular attitude was expressed about his handicap which affected me tremendously to see that here's a man who's so completely adjusted to it and the people who are working around him recognize this so that they can actually joke about it and get away with it. He enjoys it as much as they do.

> And he doesn't let his handicap give him that feeling of inferiority that some people have when they have a handicap. He doesn't have a chip on his shoulder about it. He jokes about it and so on.

The reciprocal nature of constructive attitudes toward a handicap was brought out by two colleagues:

> They don't seem handicapped. He drives a car. He drives as well as anyone else. I think that some of the confidence has come from association with people who don't consider him abnormal.

> His own personality is a clue for that (favorable attitudes). He's very patient; has a very cheerful disposition. In other words, you can't help liking him.

Three colleagues said that attitudes were, on the whole, unfavorable toward hiring deaf people like the respondents. Two of these ascribed the unfavorable feeling to difficulties of communication and the time lost thereby. One colleague was very critical of fellow workers of the respondent, ascribing their somewhat hostile attitudes to immaturity, lack of breadth and uneasiness in presence of the handicap.

Colleagues who had answered favorably were probed further with two questions. One question asked if there were any people there who were strongly favorable toward the respondent. Of the seventy so queried, thirty-six said "Yes," eighteen "No," and sixteen did not answer.

One colleague described his strongly favorable attitude with:

> I don't feel strongly favorable toward him because of his affliction. I feel strongly favorable toward him because of his capacities as a professional man. He's real sharp. He's intelligent and I admire an intelligent man. . . .

Other comments:

> I would say that all of his superiors have been favorably disposed toward him because of his loyalty, industriousness and effectiveness.
>
> He's very well liked here.
>
> He's one of the most popular people in the place.

The second question was intended to test the reaction that had preceded it by putting the problem on a concrete basis. It asked, "How do you think people would feel if there were more deaf people hired?" This question was asked of those who had, in the prior question about present attitudes toward the respondent, given neutral replies as well as those who were favorable to deaf workers. There was, in a number of cases, a more cautious attitude, arising possibly from a fear that the colleague might be committing himself for his superiors to a specific hiring policy. Table 86 shows this feeling in the large number who took a neutral view—60 per cent of the seventy-seven colleagues involved. Even these, nevertheless, were mildly favorable.

These neutral views included:

> Well, within limits, I don't think there would be any objection.
>
> As long as the person has the training to do the job and do it well, the other handicaps or idiosyncrasies don't matter.
>
> We wouldn't want to have too many. Like, say, having one in this section, one in another section . . . it wouldn't create any problem . . . (unless) it were in a section that required communication.
>
> I would say that if a person is competent, that's all that matters because all of us are handicapped in a way, you might say. . . . So if a man is competent to do a job, that's it.

TABLE 86
ATTITUDES OF CO-WORKERS TOWARD MORE DEAF
EMPLOYEES, AS FORECAST BY COLLEAGUES

Attitudes of Co-workers Toward More Deaf Employees	Number
Favorable	11
Favorable, if same as respondent	11
Neutral	46
Unfavorable	7
Did not know	1
No anwer	1
Total	77*

*From Table 85; these represent respondents toward whom co-workers had favorable or neutral attitudes, according to colleagues.

Of the twenty-two colleagues who reported favorable attitudes among co-workers, half were strongly favorable. Some reasons:

Expertness is such a rare thing in spite of all the hullabaloo that we would take anybody with two heads or no head if he could deliver. It's what you do and the way you think that counts.

If they were like him, [I'd be] glad to get them and replace some that I have.

Deaf people here are viewed as people, period.

The verdict was not always laudatory, however; some anticipated increased communication difficulties if more deaf workers were added. A number cited the few employees at the laboratory or office. As one colleague put it:

They are reluctant to take him away from me because someone else will have to break him in . . . or I mean, get used to him and his communication. So this would be a problem if we hired two or three more.

One colleague, experienced in supervising a group including seven or eight deaf workers, voiced a moderate view:

Just because they are deaf doesn't mean that they are all going to be good, doesn't mean that they are all going to be bad. . . . You get bad apples and good apples. . . .

Colleagues were also asked how respondents reacted to attitudes of friendliness. A card bearing four sentences offered them a scaled choice, as shown in Table 87.

A good many colleagues volunteered descriptive statements that the respondent was cheerful, outgoing and likable. Perhaps the one

TABLE 87

REACTIONS TO FRIENDLINESS, AS PERCEIVED BY COLLEAGUES

Reactions	Number
Tended to reject or to be suspicious of friendly overtures	2
Tended to disregard friendly overtures	1
Accepted such overtures more or less readily	42
Did not wait for friendly overtures but started them himself	40
No answer	1
Total	86*

*No colleague interview was available for one resondent.

quoted here best expressed the attitude of the eighty-two colleagues who said respondents reacted positively to friendliness:

> I don't think deafness makes a great deal of difference one way or another to her. . . . It seems to have no particular effect on her relationships with others at all. . . . She's very friendly and very happy about the whole thing.

The person discussed above was, ironically, the respondent who volunteered the following:

> In the hearing world, you need: A good command of English; the hide of an elephant; a superiority complex; an air of bravado; proper assignment of telephone calls so your subordinate won't get the notion he or she is your superior just because he or she can do it for you; a good interpreter for conferences, so you can be on the giving as well as the receiving end; a lot of common sense when meeting the public, whenever called for.

In relation to the forty respondents who were said by colleagues to start friendly overtures rather than wait for them to come from others, the comment of one respondent to a question about impatience or embarrassment of associates is pertinent:

> When I started on the job, in two or three weeks I started making friends with the people. I don't think a deaf person should wait for people to come up and make friends with him, I always went up to them and made friends and things would melt and then they would come right up to me without feeling embarrassed.

Opinions were also sought as to how respondents reacted to unfriendliness of other persons. First, however, the colleague was asked whether the respondent had ever faced the problem of a co-worker who rejected or opposed him. Only sixteen colleagues said that such a situation had occurred; fifty said it had not and the remainder (twenty-one) did not know or did not answer. Table 88 shows the colleagues' choices among five scaled statements describing possible reactions to unfriendliness. The replies were divided between two groups—those who colleagues said had experienced unfriendly attitudes and those for whom colleagues had not observed such a situation.

TABLE 88

REACTIONS OF RESPONDENTS TO UNFRIENDLINESS, AS
PERCEIVED BY COLLEAGUES

Reaction	Total	Had Experienced Unfriendliness	Had Not Experienced Unfriendliness
Aggressively rejected the other person	6	2	4
Was fearful of and disturbed by un- friendliness	9	2	7
Seemed unaware of unfriendly attitudes	8	2	6
Ignored unfriendliness, but was courte- ous	29	5	24
Strove to win an unfriendly person over	13	4	9
No answer	22	1	21
Total	87	16	71

Whether from actual experience or from conjecture, the majority of colleagues anticipated that respondents would react in an unantagonistic way, as represented by statements three to five. Reserved courtesy is the most frequent response, with twenty-nine out of the eighty-seven respondents using that approach to hostility of others.

> I think he feels fairly secure, so: "Well, if somebody doesn't like me, so what? I can live with other people; they can live without me."

> He's got a terrific sense of humor. If someone gets impatient with him, it usually ends up as a joke.

One who said this sort of situation had not occurred explained by saying:

> In the eyes of all of us who work around him, he's a perfectly normal person and I've noticed when people come in, this attitude gets across in a hurry. They, too, in just a few minutes sort of ignore his handicap and this is because they sort of forget it.

There were, however, some respondents whose adjustment to situations of strain was not so ideal. One colleague commented that his suggestion of a few years previous that the respondent try a new type of hearing aid was rejected vehemently. Another colleague described symptoms of immaturity:

> Now he is sometimes guilty of deliberately bad manners through anger. Throwing things down and walking out on people and showing violent anger on his face. . . . He's the first deaf person that I've ever encountered that has had this immaturity. Most of them are much more mature than the ordinary person in the sense of a quiet resignation to their fate and being still able to accomplish something. I've had two other cases before the respondent and nobody ever thought of their deafness.

Relations with Co-workers—Communication Difficulties

True communication—resulting in mutual understanding—is a difficult process, even for people who have all their faculties, feel goodwill and share goals. If a block is thrown into the communication pathway, irritation is likely to result. Hence, a deaf person lacking an important tool for communication must expect to experience frustration himself and to see or sense it in his associates at times. The respondents had operated successfully in environments where the potential for such frustrations must have been high.

To examine whether the respondents experienced such situations, they were asked: "Do your business associates hesitate or show reluctance when they must write to you, or repeat, or speak clearly so that you may read their lips?" Table 89 shows that forty-seven (a little more than half) of the respondents had sensed this impatience, although four out of five of them added that it occurred "sometimes," "occasionally" or "almost never."

That impatience was infrequently shown by associates is attested by replies to the question, "On the whole, would you say that most of your business associates are helpful or tolerant or impatient about

TABLE 89

IMPATIENCE OF BUSINESS ASSOCIATES AT COMMUNICATION
DIFFICULTIES, AS PERCEIVED BY RESPONDENTS

Impatience	*Number*
Impatience felt	9
Impatience felt occasionally	38
Impatience not felt	35
No answer	5
Total	87

communication?" According to Table 90, 71 per cent of the respondents rated most of their business associates as generally helpful. Only one respondent said that most of his co-workers were usually impatient.

TABLE 90

ATTITUDES OF ASSOCIATES ABOUT COMMUNICATION, AS PERCEIVED BY RESPONDENTS

Attitudes of Associates	Number
Helpful	62
Tolerant	23
Impatient	1
No answer	1
Total	87

Some respondents volunteered comments on the questions about impatience (interpreted by many to indicate discomfort or embarrassment). One has been previously quoted as advocating that the deaf person thaw the embarrassment by actively seeking friendships. Another explained how he did the same sort of thing:

> I find that when I am embarrassed, most everybody around me is embarrassed, and my long experience has gotten to the point where I treat my deafness as something in the way of an everyday experience. I've learned how to handle others who are meeting me for the first time and the situation is under control most of the time.

It is probable that these respondents and others like them interpreted the hesitation or reluctance referred to in the question as being the involuntary and barely noticeable uncertainty that a person sometimes expresses when dealing with an unknown quantity. Others probably interpreted the hesitation or reluctance as being more deliberate and noticeable. Three quotations from respondents describe the usual reactions to the latter type of impatience:

> It depends on the type of individual. If they are pleasant and friendly, they don't mind. Others are a little cold and they don't care to do it (write, speak carefully, or repeat). They're snobs and highbrows. They just don't care to take the time to write. They just don't understand deaf people. They just don't understand a handicap.

> I have very strong feelings about such people. I have not encountered it much. It is rare, very rare. They are usually small potatoes; don't amount to anything so I ignore them, brush them off. Big people don't react like that.

At first often, but after they come to know me, I never notice one bit of hesitation, unless that person is one of those that I called before "ear-centered people." They would rather listen to the radio than read a book and they would rather get all the information over a telephone than to write memos. Those people never really become understanding of the deaf. They are very rare, though.

Respondents were also asked: "How do you usually feel about the ones who are impatient?" Responses were unstructured but were categorized, as in Table 91.

TABLE 91

REACTIONS OF RESPONDENTS TO IMPATIENCE

Reaction	Number
Hostility	23
Tolerance	20
General uneasiness	17
Avoidance	8
Futility	4
Indifference	4
No experience of this sort	7
No answer	4
Total	87

The classification can be further reduced by expressing, as passive reaction, four categories—tolerance, avoidance, futility and indifference. Thirty-six (41 per cent) of the respondents expressed passive reaction. *Tolerance* applied to those respondents who expressed understanding or regret at the associates' embarrassment or spoke of ways to ease tension, such as:

I try very hard to recognize the problems that exist in any particular situation so that I may do what I can do to reduce the degree of impatience. If the impatience is justified, I try to get someone else to come in and help the impatient person to get his points across. Otherwise, I usually must insist on having the problem written so they can understand it fully.

Avoidance applied to those who said, "I try not to bother with them any more" or "Leave them conspicuously alone." *Futility* was expressed by "What can you do but let them be impatient? You have to get along with people whether they are impatient or not."

The twenty-three respondents whose replies are classified under *hostility* made such remarks as: "I get impatient, too!" One respondent was more vehement: "They must understand me and they must be patient. If they don't like it the way they found me, then I tell them to go to hell."

The term "general uneasiness" was used to describe the reactions of those who said, "I am not very comfortable myself."

Following the reply to the question about their feelings, respondents were asked, "What do you *do* about that?" Thirty-nine respondents said that they leave the impatient person alone; two of these indicated that their action was intended as a snub. Displeasure was shown more openly by four respondents, who "gave them hell" or "a sharp talking to." Efforts to help the impatient person along were related by twenty-one respondents; these efforts ranged from asking for repetition of the difficult conversation to trying to "win them over."

A situation possibly inducive to friction is one in which normal persons are supervised by one who has a handicap. At levels below professional, this sort of reaction has been frequently observed. To explore the possibility among the respondents, they were asked, "Have you ever had a job in which you supervised or gave orders to hearing persons?" Twenty-three said they had never supervised. Where the reply was affirmative, the respondent was asked, "Has anyone ever complained about you, a deaf man, giving him orders?" The interesting result from this question was that only four of the sixty-four respondents concerned reported that complaints had been made and only six sensed resistance from their subordinates. More than half (forty-six) of the total respondents said they had experienced no complaints; seven said that they did not know if complaints had been made; one did not reply.

Comments on supervising indicated that the problem of deafness in this area of working relations had been exaggerated. One respondent said: "I think that you will find that personality is more important than the lack of hearing." This same person's reaction to a subordinate's complaint was: "I am very easy-going. . . . I just let it pass. . . . After all I know my job very well."

Another respondent, long experienced in supervising, told of his coping with resistance from a subordinate: "Just being pleasant to him, trying not to offend him in any way, just respecting him and leaving him alone."

One respondent reported a different reaction from a subordinate: "In fact, one hearing man complained about another one and asked to be my assistant."

ATTITUDES ABOUT SOCIALIZING

Although the emphasis varies from firm to firm, there is a general recognition that socializing helps to lubricate the gears of the personal relationships in the working world. Socializing in an environment where hearing is the norm is not a simple matter for a deaf person, however. At a social function, the problems of expressive communication for a deaf person are greater than in an office, where all the tools of writing are readily available. Also in a strange environment, it is difficult for the deaf person to estimate the tone or volume of voice necessary to overcome surrounding noise. Another difficulty lies in the attitudes of the hearing persons present at a social gathering, described as follows by a perceptive and interested colleague of one respondent:

> People make an effort to discuss matters of technical interest in order to get the day's work done. To some, it is too much effort in a recreational setting.*

In face of the foregoing difficulties, what is the attitude of the respondents toward socializing? No direct question on attitudes was asked, but spontaneous remarks in relation to various questions ranged from:

> That's the most important thing a person can do (go to office parties). . . . Become acquainted . . . and they say, "He doesn't like us; he didn't come to the parties." . . . It's very, very necessary.

and

> Because I am deaf, I feel that if I do hold myself away from what's going on, they won't come to me either. They will put me in a corner by myself, and I don't want to stay there. I want to be just like anybody else. So I more or less force myself to be with others.

to

> We get invitations, yes. But we . . . think it is more a kindness if we don't go, because the hearing people there don't know what to do with us.

---

*This comment did not reflect the colleague's own attitude. A neighbor of the respondent, he had learned to communicate manually and had been of help in enabling the respondent to take part in community and recreational activities.

The proper conclusion probably is that individual characteristics affect these decisions quite as much as or more than deafness does of itself. The extroverts value socializing highly, whereas the introverts do not, with deafness pulling toward association with others similarly handicapped.

Despite varied attitudes, it can be seen from Table 92 that a large majority of the respondents (83 per cent) did attend office parties. Other social functions related to their work also attracted large proportions of the respondents, but of these functions only staff outings were attended by a majority.

TABLE 92

OFFICE SOCIAL FUNCTIONS ATTENDED BY RESPONDENTS

Attendance	Social Functions			
	Office Parties	*Staff Outings*	*Business Conventions*	*Other Gatherings*
Did attend	63	38	30	27
Sometimes attended	9	10	6	3
Did not attend	5	18	40	36
Did not have them	8	17	6	7
No answer	2	4	5	14
Total	87	87	87	87

Colleagues substantiated the respondents' attendance at social affairs. In seventy cases, the colleagues said that the respondents attended office social affairs. Fifty-two attended as often as or more often than hearing fellow workers. Some respondents were observed by colleagues to be taking part in other company activities: twelve in athletics, five in hobbies, one in Boy Scout work.

Thirty-six attended business conventions and forty did not. Six firms did not involve such occasions. These proportions compare with those observed in Chapter VI on professional meetings. One respondent felt that he should be sent to such meetings by his firm and had a *modus operandi* to meet objections about communication difficulties:

> I talked to my boss and I explained to him that I felt I was more qualified to go to those conventions and I told him that in every big city in the United States I had several people who can interpret for me. I would be very happy to avail myself of these opportunities to the exent of paying for the services of these interpreters.

It may be said that the respondents as a group participated freely in the social activities of the firms for which they worked. Another question arises: Did they carry this association further into the area of socializing for relaxation and recreation? Many deaf persons make the effort to associate with people who hear to the extent of necessary business contacts but for relaxation and recreation prefer the company of other deaf persons and the ease of communication in the sign language.

Respondents were asked whether they visited the homes of their colleagues and whether these colleagues visited the respondents' homes. Their replies are shown in Table 93.

TABLE 93

VISITS BY COLLEAGUES TO RESPONDENTS' HOMES AND BY
RESPONDENTS TO COLLEAGUES' HOMES, AS PERCEIVED
BY RESPONDENTS

	By Colleagues to Respondents	*By Respondents to Colleagues*
Did visit	36	39
Visited, but rarely	20	19
Not done here	5	6
Did not visit	25	22
No answer	1	1
Total	87	87

About 40 to 45 per cent of the respondents did visit and entertain their colleagues; around 22 per cent did so rarely; about 25 per cent did not visit.

Colleagues were asked about visits also and additionally were asked to compare the frequency of such visits with those of their co-workers who could hear. Table 94 presents the replies:

Around a third of the colleagues reported that they and the respondents visited each other at home. A larger number of colleagues, about 45 per cent, reported that such visiting was not done among employees of that firm. Almost 20 per cent of the respondents visited their colleagues more frequently than did other business associates of the colleagues.

It might be asked with whom the respondents did visit, other than business associates. Some inkling of the nature of their purely social lives was given in Table 7 showing means of communication used

TABLE 94

FREQUENCY OF VISITS BY COLLEAGUES TO RESPONDENTS'
HOMES AND BY RESPONDENTS TO COLLEAGUES' HOMES,
AS PERCEIVED BY COLLEAGUES

| | *Visits* | |
Frequency of Visits	*By Colleagues to Respondents*	*By Respondents to Colleagues*
More often than other workers	12	17
As often	14	14
As often (qualified)*	38	41
Less often	8	5
Never	6	4
No answer	9	6
Total	87	87

*"As often, which is never," or "as often but nobody does it here."

when not at work. Another measure of socializing is an index of association with people who hear, which was constructed from answers to six questions used in this study. The six questions dealt with membership in organizations, association with business associates off the job and association with deaf persons. They were weighted and combined to provide a scale of $+12$ to -12 and these values were further consolidated into the frequencies indicated in Table 95. The index is also described in Appendix F.

TABLE 95

FREQUENCY OF ASSOCIATION WITH PEOPLE WHO HEAR

Frequency of Association	*Number*	*Per Cent*
Very frequent	18	21
Frequent	30	34
Average	9	10
Less frequent	27	31
Rare	3	3
Total	87	99

If this index is a valid measure, then it is apparent that more than half of the respondents associated frequently with hearing persons and very few did so rarely. The index corresponds inversely to the proportion of social time spent with deaf friends as may be seen from Table 96.

It is not to be expected that a deaf person will have absolutely no social contacts with people who hear; there are relatives, friends, neighbors, fellow workers; with them, he will associate at least to a minimum. Respondents' off-the-job associations tended to correspond, by and large, to the indications of the association index.

TABLE 96

FREQUENCY OF ASSOCIATION WITH PEOPLE WHO HEAR, BY
PROPORTION OF OFF-THE-JOB SOCIAL CONTACTS WITH
DEAF PEOPLE

Frequency of Association	Proportion of Off-the-job Social Contacts with Deaf People						
	Total	All	More than half	Half	Less than half	Few	None
Very frequent	18				5	9	4
Frequent	30		11	4	5	7	3
Average	9		5	1	1	1	1
Less frequent	27	2	20	2	2		1
Rare	3	1	2				
Total	87	3	38	7	13	17	9

Are those persons who associate socially most often with other deaf persons more or less conscious of their deafness than are those who seek the company of people who can hear? Comparison of the proportion of social contacts with deaf persons and the index of salience of deafness* in Table 97 gives an inconclusive picture, with those who associate more frequently with hearing persons tending slightly more often to have a lower salience of deafness.

Respondents who spent less than half of their social hours with other deaf people included more of those skilled in speech and lip-reading than did the group who spent more than half their social time with other deaf persons, as is shown in Table 98.

The cause-and-effect relationship in the above data is not clear. Did those skilled in speech and lipreading find it easier to socialize with hearing persons than those less skilled? Or did frequent association with hearing people sharpen their communication skills?

Respondents were asked to explain why they associated in the

TABLE 97

PROPORTION OF OFF-THE-JOB SOCIAL CONTACTS WITH DEAF
PERSONS, BY SALIENCE OF DEAFNESS

Salience of Deafness	Proportion of Social Contacts with Deaf People	
	Half or More Per Cent	Less than Half Per Cent
Low	61	69
High	39	31
Total	100	100

---

*See Appendix E for a description of the index.

TABLE 98

PROPORTION OF OFF-THE-JOB CONTACTS WITH DEAF PEOPLE,
BY SPEECH SKILLS

Speech Skills	Proportion of Social Contacts with Deaf People	
	Half or More Per Cent	*Less than Half Per Cent*
Expressive—associates understood:		
Almost everything said or better	70	84
Occasional word or less	30	16
Total	100	100
Receptive—respondent understood:		
Short conversation or better	50	76
Simple sentence or less	50	24
Total	100	100

proportions which they did. As Table 99 indicates, the chief reasons
for choosing to associate more frequently with deaf people were an
affinity for others similarly handicapped and a desire for social relations without the strain of speech and lipreading. Those who associated more often with hearing persons most frequently gave no special
reason; there were some who found hearing people more stimulating;
a few clung to family and childhood ties.

TABLE 99

REASONS FOR ASSOCIATIONS OFF-THE-JOB

Reasons	*Number*
More than half of contacts with deaf persons:	(49)
Affinity for deaf persons	18
Ease of association (less strain)	10
Better communication through sign language	5
Desire to serve deaf people	6
Family and social ties	2
Imposition on those who can hear	2
No special reason	6
Less than half of contacts with deaf persons:	(40)
Hearing people are more stimulating	10
Family and childhood ties	5
Too busy or too tired	4
Other	8*
No special reason	13
Associations half and half	7
No answer	4
Total	100†

*3 did not know sign language; 1 each: job requires it, mutual interests with
co-workers, few deaf people in neighborhood, association with deaf persons
would remind respondent of his handicap.
† Total exceeds 87 because of multiple answers.

Finally, there is the more formal type of socializing evidenced by membership in organizations. The respondents were asked about memberships in organizations of two communities, that of their residence and that of deaf people. Among the eighty-seven respondents, there were two hundred forty memberships in one or another type of organization of and for the deaf and 153 memberships in community organizations. Ten respondents belonged to no organization of the deaf; twenty-five respondents belonged to no community organizations. Memberships in four or more organizations for deaf people were held by thirty-six respondents; sixteen respondents belonged to four or more community organizations. Most popular types of organizations for the deaf were alumni associations (48 per cent) and fraternal organizations (43 per cent). Among community organizations, hobby groups attracted 41 per cent of the respondents and church-connected organizations, 30 per cent.

TABLE 100

TYPES OF ORGANIZATIONS TO WHICH RESPONDENTS BELONG

Type of Organization	Number	Per Cent of Total Respondents
Organizations of the deaf:		
National Association of the Deaf	32	37
State Associations of the Deaf	32	37
City group	10	11
Hearing society	4	5
Social club	34	39
Fraternal organizations	37	43
Church-connected group	27	31
Alumni association	42	48
Other	12*	14
None	10	11
Total	240†	—†
Community organizations:		
Parent-Teacher association	21	24
Citizens association	15	17
Fraternal organization	6	7
Church-connected group	26	30
Service club	2	2
Hobby club	36	41
Alumni association	13	15
Other	9‡	10
None	25	29
Total	153†	—†

*Recreational, 6; investment, 3; professional oral deaf, 2; fraternal, 1.

† Totals exceed 87 and 100 per cent because of multiple answers.

‡ Scout work, 4; recreational, 3; political, 1; Toastmasters Club, 1.

SUMMARY

The respondents indicated reasonable satisfaction with their lives as self-evaluated, but a majority felt that they would have achieved more if they could hear. Yet deafness was not a highly salient aspect of their thought; as revealed by free answers to seven of the questions which could have involved deafness, over half of the respondents mentioned their deafness in only two of the seven questions.

They were a job-oriented group of people and were often characterized as keen and competent workers. Their relations with co-workers were seen as friendly by 95 per cent of their colleagues. Business associates held favorable attitudes toward 80 per cent of these deaf workers, strongly favorable to 42 per cent of them. Respondents had experienced occasional impatience from associates over communication difficulties, but on the whole eighty-five of the eighty-seven respondents characterized attitudes of their business associates toward communication difficulties as helpful or tolerant.

A majority of the respondents attended office parties and similar employee gatherings. Less than half of them attended business or professional meetings. About two thirds of the respondents visited back and forth with colleagues, although this aspect of relations among the workers was generally discounted by both the respondents and the colleagues.

About three-fifths of the respondents reported that half or more of their social contacts after working hours were with deaf people. This preference was attributed by the majority to affinity for other deaf people and to ease of communication. Three respondents said that all of their social contacts were with deaf people and nine reported no contacts with deaf persons. Skill in speech and lipreading was related to infrequency of social contacts with deaf people. The more frequent socializing with deaf people showed up in organization memberships. Memberships in organizations of deaf people totaled 240; in general community organizations, 153. The organizations of the deaf most frequently joined were alumni organizations, fraternal and social groups and special interest civic organizations. Among the community organizations, the most frequently joined were hobby clubs, church-connected groups and parent-teacher associations.

Chapter IX

SUMMARY

THE STUDY WAS undertaken with three general goals: (1) To augment existing, mainly popular, information about the occupational status of deaf people; (2) to broaden for rehabilitation counselors, social workers and educators the traditional view about deaf workers to include not just the problem cases but also persons with optimal achievement; (3) to examine systematically the problems, experiences and abilities of deaf persons in professional employment. It was also hoped that the study might provide clues for further, more detailed research.

The basis for the study consists of interviews with eighty-seven deaf persons employed for three years or longer in occupations classified by the Bureau of Census as "professional, technical and kindred." Excluded, however, were professionals acting as independent agents and those serving chiefly deaf people. All respondents were deaf to the extent that communication was received by them visually—by writing, by lipreading and/or by the sign language.

COMMUNICATION

A majority of the respondents depended mainly upon oral communication at their places of employment; 63 per cent of the eighty-seven respondents used oral means for expression and 55 per cent for reception as compared to 35 and 40 per cent who used writing as their most frequent means of communication.

It is probable that the ability to communicate through speech and lipreading was associated with their occupational accomplishments. Specifically how the skill is related was not explored, but speculation would point to the resulting facility in day-to-day contacts and possibly to more ready acceptance by co-workers because these respondents seemed more normal than those who did not communicate orally at all.

[155]

These statements above do not necessarily mean that the respondents shunned manual communication. In relations with their deaf friends, 80 per cent of the respondents used manual communication. Also the preferences of the respondents were not so strong for oral communication at work as their use of it. Although 61 per cent preferred speech for expression, only 40 per cent preferred to receive through lipreading. Almost half of these lip-readers preferred writing when a conversation was complex or technical.

Skill in carrying on an oral conversation probably affected the respondents' preferences for means of communication. According to the respondents' evaluations, three fourths of them could speak well enough for their hearing associates to understand almost everything the respondents said; in lipreading, however, only 21 per cent of the respondents could understand almost everything said by associates. Colleagues rated the respondents higher in their speech and lipreading, ascribing the same abilities to 80 and 43 per cent of the respondents, respectively. The rating in speech was pushed higher by the thirty-four respondents whose deafness occurred after age six, when a good basic ability in speech had been acquired. The lipreading of these thirty-four did not rate highly; only six said they could understand almost everything their colleagues said.

In short, it may be said that almost all of the respondents used speech to some extent in their business relationships, but many of them would have preferred to use other means of communication and had less than full confidence in their oral communication abilities, especially in lipreading.

AGE OF OCCURRENCE OF DEAFNESS

A finding of significance, especially to educators, concerned the age at which deafness occurred. Educators of deaf people generally agree that language is the great problem in educating deaf people and that the lack of stimulation through the ear severely limits language development during the early years. These facts plus the need of clear expression in most professions would indicate that deaf professional workers would come chiefly from among those deafened during late youth. This view is substantiated to some extent in this study. Nevertheless, a significant 52 per cent of the respondents became deaf before age six. Thirty per cent of respondents were born deaf compared to 28.5 per cent of those studied in the *Survey of Occupational Conditions Among the Deaf.*[2] Jarvik *et al.* also found a ratio of deaf-born to total population of 30.4 among male achievers and 36.9 among the total male population of New York State.[8] The implications of these early deafened respondents' achievements should be recognized by educators as of encouraging importance in regard to curricula, methods and philosophies of education. In short, this finding denies the too prevalent negative attitude that a person born deaf is so deeply handicapped that significant educational and professional accomplishment is not possible for him. Instead, educators should be constantly aware that each deaf individual may possess those qualities of mind and personality which might allow them to progress to levels of accomplishment exemplified by these respondents. Encouraging in this direction is current research on cognition, language acquisition and early education of deaf children.

EDUCATION

There was no strongly predominant educational pattern among these respondents. A variety of schools and educational methods were represented. From ninety-five collegiate institutions, sixty-one respondents (over 70 per cent) had earned degrees, twenty-two of which were beyond the bachelor's degree. Doctorates had been earned by five respondents, three of whom had been deafened before age six. Difficulties encountered by the respondents while attending regular colleges and universities included the securing of lecture notes, participation in seminars and consultation with their professors. However, most of the respondents reported their troubles at college as not of great moment.

ENTRY INTO CAREER

Occupational selections were made by roughly equal proportions of the respondents during early childhood, adolescence, college years and their working period. Sources of information were cited as the chief (first named) factor in selection of occupations by a majority of respondents, but when all factors were considered, self-attributes were mentioned oftenest with interest as the most frequent and deafness next. Yet only six of them gave precedence to deafness as the first factor in their career selection.

The leading problem faced in securing the first job was discrimination, yet only a third of the respondents reported that they actually were discriminated against. In overcoming possible resistance to employing them, a third person was a catalyst for 65 per cent of the job applicants. This area of job-seeking seemed to be the biggest hurdle these deaf workers encountered. One of the respondents suggested a career clinic to travel to schools and provide expert advice and guidance to young deaf people in their vocational aspirations and decisions. Certainly the coming crisis in placement which will arise from the demands of automation and deficiencies in their education requires careful study, pertinent training and selective placement of deaf youth.

OCCUPATIONS AND ECONOMIC POSITIONS

The respondents were employed in twenty-nine different occupations, most of them laboratory or desk jobs. This concentration in laboratory and office work results in part from the selection process of this study which excluded independent agents and teachers and ministers serving deaf people. It probably represents also an avoidance by deaf workers of occupations requiring ready or expert communication, such as law, medicine, sales and the like.

Incomes of the respondents were high, the median of $7,615 per year being greater than that of professional workers fourteen years of age and over in the general population in 1960. This latter group, however, included teaching and the ministry, two generally low-paid professions. High incomes tended to go to the men, scientists, skilled users of speech, the more highly educated, and those deafened after the age of six years.

ON-THE-JOB PROBLEMS

The use of the telephone and participation in group discussions were the two largest problems for these deaf professional workers. Ingenuity by the deaf person and accommodation by co-workers alleviated these difficulties to an extent, but all the respondents realized that advancement to levels where communication becomes a large part of the job was not to be expected. Despite these difficulties, hearing colleagues rated the performance of 90 per cent of the respondents as good as or better than that of their co-workers.

The respondents were found to be very stable workers. Three fourths of them had held four jobs or fewer during their careers and over a quarter of them had been at the same job all their working lives. Bigman's [2] venture that fear of prejudice in a new job made deaf people reluctant to change jobs probably holds true with many of these respondents.

ATTITUDES ABOUT DEAFNESS

Most of the respondents were reasonably well satisfied with their achievements, although most also felt that they would have accomplished more if they could hear. They were mostly job-oriented people and were rated as keen and competent workers by their colleagues. Relationships with their co-workers were generally good; most co-workers felt favorable toward them probably because of the friendly attitudes of the respondents. Communication problems did not create much friction; all but two of the respondents reported their associates as being tolerant or helpful about them.

Respondents socialized about as much as their co-workers, both on and off the job. There was some social interchange between the respondents and their co-workers. However, about three fifths of the respondents spent half or more of their off-the-job social hours with other deaf people because of affinity and a greater ease of communication. Those who socialized more frequently with people who could hear said that they did so mainly because they found hearing people more stimulating. Speech skills were found to be related to association with hearing people.

An outstanding characteristic revealed in this section seems to be friendliness and ability to get along with people, an attribute of greatest value in the close relationships that exist in our daily working environment.

IN GENERAL

Perhaps a significant finding of the study is that, other than personal competence and drive, there seems to have been no single determinant of success for these deaf people in professional employment. Skill in speech and lipreading was a frequent factor, but there were a number of respondents who never used them and more who were not particularly skilled, especially in reception. Numerous educational patterns were involved, from nonspecialized schooling to an education secured entirely from the residential schools for the deaf. Varied approaches to job seeking prevailed, though many used a third party to break down resistance. The problems which the respondents met on the job were very much the same for all of them and they met them in a variety of ways. In short, deaf people are people, and as such their talents and accomplishments will vary.

IMPLICATIONS FOR RESEARCH AND TRAINING

These findings point to no one specific conclusion. The study was designed rather to provide a general picture of deaf persons in professional employment. However, from it can be drawn a number of implications which apply to the training of deaf people and to further research about them.

Of very great importance in any social research about deaf people would be a careful examination of the communication process. It was surprising to find in preliminary reading how few researchers had offered really useful information about how deaf people communicated. In the *Survey of Occupational Conditions Among the Deaf,* for instance, the respondents were asked to report which of several means of communication were used with co-workers, but no provision was made to indicate the extent to which the respondents used each means. Nor were they asked which method they preferred to use. In this study, the various methods of communication were ranked as to frequency of use and thus could be cross-tabulated with other replies.

Likewise, the *Survey* queries about lipreading ability were vague—for example, "enough to understand conversation" but not what sort of conversation or how long it lasted. The present study made a rough scale of comprehension for both receptive and expressive communication. This is an area where teachers of speech could do some analyzing to provide researchers with an adequate scale of speech comprehension and use.

Another area of speech where research could be profitable is that of electronic translating devices for those persons for whom hearing aids bear no promise. The simple meter recently devised for use with the telephone is an example of ingenuity applied to a problem of communication.

The large percentage of deaf-born and early deafened respondents in this group of professional people should be an encouraging phenomenon to all educators of the deaf. It indicates that such a deaf person has as great a potential for learning as has any other and if it is properly tapped and given encouragement, the result can be educational accomplishment in the highest bracket. Present research in cognition, early language acquisition and early formal education holds promise of a more stimulating and more purposeful educational environment for the very young deaf child.

Related to such research might be studies to find the optimal age for beginning instruction in speech and lipreading. Educators have long assumed that it is necessary to subject the very young deaf child to a stringent oral environment so that he could acquire proficiency in speech and lipreading. This is an assumption. It needs to be tested. Another possible assumption is that the deaf child should not attempt to read the lips until he has the vocabulary to comprehend and the maturity to understand the purpose of what he is attempting. This, too, needs to be tested.

An investigation might be made in the direction of aids needed by deaf students in regular colleges and universities. Perhaps the studies currently being made by the University of Illinois will be productive. There have been isolated instances where deaf students were provided with an interpreter or an amanuensis to aid with lectures and discussion classes. More than that is needed, however. College is a social experience and as much growth occurs outside the classroom as does within. Deaf students, like their hearing peers, need counseling in their social problems as well as help in the classroom.

The questions about occupational choice and job-seeking were rather general. The whole area needs closer examination and young deaf people, restricted as they are in casual acquisition of such knowledge, badly need occupational information. Perhaps less time devoted by schools for the deaf to training in the mechanics of trades would allow more time to learn of the great variety of occupations existing. One respondent suggested a team to travel among the schools for the deaf, giving instruction in occupational opportunities and how to seek them.

The deaf person's on-the-job situation is another fruitful area of research for the social researcher. As regards professional workers, he might investigate, in greater depth than here, the mobility of deaf workers, both in the firm and in the labor market: How they have been promoted and why; whether their stability stems from professional commitment or from uneasiness at the prospect of a new working environment; whether there really does exist a ceiling upon advancement and at what level. This area of work attitudes and relationships could be a fascinating, though difficult, study for a sociologist or a psychologist.

The character of a deaf person's social life is another fruitful area of research as is becoming recognized today. Study should be made of not only the deaf person's social attitudes, but also those of his hearing friends, neighbors and co-workers.

Encouraging as regards the whole field of behavioral research about deafness was the National Research Conference on Behavioral Aspects of Deafness held in New Orleans, May 3-5, 1965. There were gathered at this meeting about seventy persons who were engaged in research on deafness or a related area. Five years ago, it might have been difficult to gather a dozen such researchers. Numbers, of course, do not insure quality of results, but the growth of interest indicates surely that the field is a fertile one.

BIBLIOGRAPHY

1. *American Annals of the Deaf, 106*:1, January, 1961.
2. BIGMAN, STANLEY K., and LUNDE, ANDERS S.: *Occupational Conditions Among the Deaf.* Washington, D. C., Gallaudet College, 1959.
3. BLOCK, SAMUEL A.: Attitudes of management toward college-trained deaf workers in government. *Gallaudet Coll Bull, 2*(2):27-32, October, 1955.
4. BRUNSMAN, HOWARD G.: *Alphabetical Index of Occupations and Industries.* Washington, D. C., Bureau of the Census, Department of Commerce, 1950.
5. CARR-SAUNDERS, A. M. in FISHER, ROBERT M.: *The Metropolis in Modern Life.* New York, Doubleday and Co., 1955.
6. DUBIN, ROBERT: *The World of Work.* Englewood Cliffs, New Jersey, Prentice-Hall, 1958.
7. EDWARDS, ALBA M.: *A Social-Economic Grouping of the Gainful Workers of the United States.* Washington, D. C., Government Printing Office, 1938.
8. JARVIK, LISSY FEINGOLD; SALZER, ROSA M., and FALEK, ARTHUR: Deaf persons of outstanding achievement. In RAINIER, JOHN; ALTSHULER, KENNETH Z., and KALLMAN, FRANZ D. (EDS.): *Family and Mental Health Problems in a Deaf Population.* New York, Columbia University, 1963.
9. LIPSET, F. M., and MALM, F. T.: First jobs and career patterns. *American Journal of Economics and Sociology, 14*:247-261, April, 1955.
10. MARTENS, ELISE H.: *The Deaf and the Hard-of-Hearing in the Occupational World.* Washington, D. C., Government Printing Office, 1937.
11. MILLER, DELBERT C., and FORM, WILLIAM H.: *Industrial Sociology.* New York, Harper and Brothers, c 1951.
12. SCHOWE, BEN M.: The alumni lectures of 1955. *Gallaudet Coll Bull, 4*:2, October, 1955.
13. SCHOWE, BEN M.: Unpublished letter, December 23, 1956.
14. SMITH, MAPHEUS: Occupational mobility of notable persons. *Sociology and Social Research, 23*:503-513, July-August, 1939.
15. United States Department of Commerce, Bureau of the Census: *Current Population Reports, Consumer Income.* Series P-60, No. 37, July 17, 1962.
16. United States Department of Commerce, Bureau of the Census: *United States Census of Population, 1960, 1*:1. Washington, D. C., Government Printing Office, 1962.
17. UTLEY, JEAN: *Teachers' Lesson Manual for the 16mm Motion Picture, "How Well Can You Read the Lips?"* Chicago, DeVry Corporation, 1111 Armitage Avenue, n.d.

APPENDICES

APPENDIX A

THE SELECTION PROCEDURE

Letter Soliciting Participation

Dear Sir:

As you probably know from experience, those of us who are deaf and who aspire to professional employment must learn to deal with many problems arising from our deafness. How best to use the telephone, to participate in group conferences or to meet the public? Can you gain the respect and confidence of your associates by professional competence alone, or is there more to it than that? Is there a ceiling imposed by deafness?

Probably you will be quick to see the value of answers to such questions for occupational counselors, educators and young deaf people being trained for the more responsible types of employment. To inquire into this field, Gallaudet College is sponsoring a research project with the help of a generous grant from the US Office of Vocational Rehabilitation. With the aid of a group of 100 deaf persons who, like you, have been through the mill, the study will seek to identify and examine such problems as we have mentioned. Could you give us the benefit of your experience for this purpose?

There will be a personal interview which will probably take a couple of hours of your time. In addition, we would like to interview your employer or a colleague to get management's views about the deaf in professional work.

Your confidence in answering questions will be scrupulously respected. All information will be identified only by code number and the names associated with code numbers will be known only to the interviewer and the study director. Identities will be masked in the final report.

You have been suggested to us as one in the kind of employment which we want to study. It would help, however, if you would answer the questions on the sheet enclosed to clear up this point. Please mail one of the copies to us (the other is for your file). When we have heard from you, we shall write again about a date for the interview. We hope you will help with this study. The experience should be interesting.

Our interviewer is available only until mid-September and scheduling his visits takes some time, so an early reply to this letter will be very much appreciated.

Yours very truly,

Alan B. Crammatte, Director

Questionnaire Sent to Prospective Respondents

In order that the material collected for this study will be comparable and the study group clearly defined, there are criteria of age, professional status, stability of employment and deafness. Your answers to these questions will help us to select comparable participants.

1. Are you able to hear and understand spoken conversation either with or without a hearing aid?　——　Yes　——　No*
2. If your answer was "No" to Question 1, at what age did you become completely unable to hear and understand conversation?
3. What is the title of your occupation?
4. Please describe your duties briefly.
5. For how many years have you worked at this occupation?
6. For how many years have you worked for this company?
7. Is your salary $4,000 or over per year? —— Under $4,000, —— (check one)
8. We must schedule interviews for the summer time, when most people take their vacations. It will help us a great deal on a complicated job if you would write below the dates when you do *not* expect to be available for an interview.
9. In preparing our interview and questions, we have tried to anticipate some of the problems you may have encountered in your work. However, we certainly do not feel that we know all there is to know about adjustment of the deaf to their occupations. If you have ideas on the general subject of problems of adjustment to your job and to your hearing co-workers, we would like very much to know them before our interviewer goes out among you. Very likely your suggestions could direct the interviewer into useful channels. Hence, if the spirit moves you to share your ideas on this subject, just use this page and the blank sheet which is attached to these questions.

Alternate Question 1

1. For the study group we wish to make a very careful selection as regards ability to hear. For this purpose we are using the rating scale below. Reading down from the top, please find *the description that best describes* your maximum hearing ability in your usual contact with hearing people. After you have selected the description that best fits, check *one* of the blanks to the right of that description to indicate whether this best hearing is accomplished with or without a hearing aid. Check only *one* blank.

---

*This question was considerably expanded after the first 100 questionnaires had been returned. A copy of the new questions follows this questionnaire.

	With *Hearing Aid*	*Without* *Hearing Aid*
(a) I cannot hear any sounds.	——	——
(b) I can hear loud sounds but cannot identify the nature of the sounds heard.	——	——
(c) I can identify the nature of the sounds I hear but cannot understand words without the aid of lipreading.	——	——
(d) I can understand some words through hearing alone but I cannot succeed in an extended direct conversation without the aid of lipreading.	——	——
(e) I can understand an extended conversation without relying on lipreading.	——	——
(f) I can converse on the telephone.	——	——

2. At what age did the condition you selected in answer to Question 1 occur?

APPENDIX B

COLLEGES AND UNIVERSITIES ATTENDED
BY THE RESPONDENTS

Akron University
American University
Antioch College
Armour Institute of Technology
Bridgeport Engineering Institute
Brooklyn Law School
Bureau of Standards Graduate School
Butler University
California Institute of Technology
Carnegie Tech
Case Institute of Technology
Catholic University of America
City College of San Francisco
Clark University
Clemson University
College of the City of New York
Columbia University
Department of Agriculture
  Graduate School
Drexel Institute of Technology
Duke University
Eastern Illinois State College
Eastern Michigan University
El Camino Junior College
Elmhurst College
Evansville College
Fairleigh Dickinson College
Fordham University
Gallaudet College
George Washington University
Grinnell College
Heald Engineering College
Illinois Institute of Technology
Institute of Applied Arts and Sciences
  (University of the State of
  New York)
Iowa State University

John Marshall Law School
Johns Hopkins University
Kings College
Lafayette College
Lawrence College
Lewis Institute, Chicago
Los Angeles City College
Louisiana State University
Lowell Technological Institute
Lyons Township Junior College
Manhattan College
Marquette University
Mars Hill Junior College
New Mexico State University
New York University
North Park College
North Texas State College
Northwestern University
Notre Dame University
Occidental College
Ohio State University
Pennsylvania State University
Pierce Junior College
Princeton University
Queens College (New York)
Rhode Island School of Design
Roosevelt University
San Diego State College
Southern Methodist University
Swarthmore College
Temple University
Texas A. and M. College
Tri-State College (Indiana)
University of Alabama
University of Alaska
University of California
University of Chicago

University of Cincinnati
University of the City of Los Angeles
University of Georgia
University of Illinois
University of Maryland
University of Michigan
University of Pennsylvania
University of Pittsburgh
University of Southern California
University of Texas
University of Utah

University of Wisconsin
Wabash College
Washington State College
Washington University (St. Louis)
Wayne University
Weber College
Westminster College
Whittworth College
Wilkes College
Yale University
Ypsilanti Teachers College

APPENDIX C

EMPLOYERS

American Cyanamid Company
American Smelting and Refining Company, Dept. of Agricultural Research
Anheuser-Busch, Inc.
Armour Research Foundation
Bell Telephone Company Laboratories
Biochemical Research Foundation
Cellarius and Hilmer, Architects
Central Farmers Fertilizer Company
Charles F. Kettering Foundation
Chance Vought Aircraft Company
Colorado School of Mines Research Foundation
Columbia University
Engineering Consultation, Inc.
E. I. DuPont de Nemours Company
Eaton Manufacturing Company
Firestone Tire and Rubber Company (*3 respondents*)
D. H. Litter and Company
Frank L. Hope, Architect
General Dynamics, Convair Division (*2 respondents*)
Hispanic Society of America (*3 respondents*)
Hydro-Aire, Inc.
Indiana State Board of Health
James Forestal Research Center
Johns Hopkins University, Applied Physics Laboratory
Julien Collins Company
Lockheed Aircraft Company
Los Angeles Bureau of Engineering, Public Works
Los Angeles Bureau of Engineering, Street Opening and Widening Division
Inland-Magill-Weinsumer Corporation
Major-Monroe Dental Laboratory
Marquardt Corporation
Martin Company
Martin Sternberg Associates
Michigan Employment Security Commission
Monsanto Chemical Company
New York State Department of Labor and Industry
New York University, Bellevue Medical Center
North American Aviation, Inc.

North American Aviation, Inc., Rocketdyne Division (*3 respondents*)
Ogden (Utah) City Engineering Department
Olin Matheson, Acousta Paper Division
Oschner Foundation Research Laboratory
Perkins-Elmer Company
Pitney Bowes Company
Radio Corporation of America, West Coast Missile and Surface Radar Division
Ray O. Peck and Val Brennan, Architects
Rexall Drug Company
Russell Library
Sears, Roebuck and Company
Smith-Emery Company
Sulphite Pulp Manufacturers Research League
Sun Oil Company
United States Government (*24 respondents*)
    Department of Agriculture:
        Agricultural Research Service
        Eastern Utilization Research and Development Division
        Forest Service
        Marketing Administrative Service
    Department of Commerce:
        Bureau of the Census
        Bureau of Standards
        Geological Survey
        Patent Office
        Weather Bureau
    Department of Defense:
        Air Force
        Army Map Service
        Corps of Engineers
        Navy
        Quartermaster Corps
        White Sands Missile Range
    Department of Health, Education, and Welfare:
        Office of Vocational Rehabilitation
    Federal Power Commission
    Housing and Home Finance Administration
    Railroad Retirement Board
United States Steel Company, Research Center (*2 respondents*)
Wenger Laboratories
David T. Witherly, Engineers
World Publishing Company
Wright Aeronautical Division

APPENDIX D

PROFESSIONAL ORGANIZATIONS HAVING RESPONDENTS AS MEMBERS

Akron Rubber Group
Alpha Chi Sigma
American Accounting Association (*2 respondents; 1 resigned*)
American Association for the Advancement of Science (*4 respondents*)
American Association for Clinical Chemists
American Association of Textile Chemists
American Bar Association
American Chemical Society (*22 respondents; 4 resigned*)
American Geophysical Union
American Institute of Certified Public Accountants
    (*2 respondents; 1 resigned*)
American Institute of Chemists
American Institute of Architects
American Institute of Nutrition
American Library Association (*2 respondents; 1 resigned*)
American Meteorological Society
American Pharmaceutical Association
American Public Health Association
American Rocket Society
American Society of Civil Engineers
American Society of Microbiology
American Society of Parasitology (*resigned*)
American Society for Testing Materials
American Statistical Association (*2 respondents*)
Art Students League
Chicago Bar Association
Cincinnati Architectural Society
Consumer Finance Association
Development Engineering
Educational Writers Association
Federated Societies of Sewerage and Industrial Wastes
Illinois Bar Association
Illinois Society of Certified Public Accountants
Association of American Bacteriologists (Indiana Branch)
Institute of Food Technologists
Institute of Aeronautical Scientists
International Union for the Scientific Study of Population

Metropolitan Chemical Society
Michigan Society of Registered Land Surveyors
Michigan State Board of Registered Architects,
    Professional Engineers and Land Surveyors
Monsanto Management Club
National Association of Accountants
National Association of Claimants
National Association of Clinical Labs
National Rehabilitation Association
National Vocational Guidance Association (*resigned*)
Needle and Bobbin Club of New York City
New York Academy of Sciences (*3 respondents*)
Ogden (Utah) Engineers Club (*2 respondents*)
Optical Society of America (*resigned*)
Phi Lambda Epsilon
Population Association of America
Poultry Science Association
Public Relations Society of America
Research Society of America
Rho Chi
Sigma Xi (*4 respondents*)
Society of Agronomy
Society of American Bacteriologists
Society for Applied Spectroscopists
Society of Automotive Engineers
Society for Industrial Microbiology
Society of Professional Employees
Special Libraries Association
Technical Association of the Pulp and Paper Industry
Texas Surveyors Association
Trial Lawyers Club of Chicago
Wisconsin Academy of Science

APPENDIX E

INDEX OF SALIENCE OF DEAFNESS

As a rough indication of how greatly deafness colored the thoughts of the respondents in relation to their occupations and their success in life, an index of salience of deafness was constructed. Certain questions involving deafness, but not mentioning deafness or in any way guiding the respondent's thinking in that direction were examined for any spontaneous reference to deafness, hearing or any other aspect of the handicap. The questions were coded for (1) mention by the respondent of deafness or related matters in *any* way, (2) no mention of deafness or related matters, (3) no answer. No determination of weight to be put on the questions was made.

In constructing the index, mention of deafness in any one question was scored 1; no mention or no answer was scored 0. The index was determined by the total score of each respondent, for example, a respondent who mentioned deafness in any three of the questions received an index number of 3. An index of 7 indicates a very high awareness of deafness, while an index of 0 represents the lowest salience of deafness.

The questions:

> How did you happen to become a *(occupation)?*
>
> Did you make a deliberate choice of your kind of work or did you get into the work more or less by chance?
>
> In your opinion, why have you moved around from job to job so (often, seldom)?
>
> How would you describe the very best way of life for a person like you?
>
> How would you describe the very worst way of life for a person like you?
>
> You have described and rated goals and achievements in terms of "a person like you." When you answered those questions, what kind of a person were you thinking about?
>
> Can you recall any childhood ambitions (or experiences) that might have influenced your choice (of a career)?

INDEX OF ASSOCIATION WITH PERSONS WHO HEAR

Since several of the questions dealt with socializing with business associates and other hearing persons and one with social contacts with deaf persons, six such questions were combined to form a rough indicator of how frequently the respondents socialized with hearing people. This was termed the index of association with persons who hear. The questions used and the weights given to the replies are listed below:

	Weights				
	+2	+1	0	−1	−2
About what proportion of your social contacts off the job are with other deaf persons?	Few or none	Less than half	Half	More than half	All
. . . tell me how many of such organizations (of and for the deaf) you belong to.	none or 1	2	3	4	5 or more
Tell me . . . to how many (community organizations) you belong.	4 or more	3	2	1	none
Do you attend office parties?	Yes		Don't have them	Rarely	No
Do business associates visit you at your home?	Yes		Not done here	Rarely	No
Do you visit business associates?	Yes		Not done here	Rarely	No

The largest possible scores are +12 and −12. The range +7 to +12 was taken to indicate very frequent association with hearing persons; +1 to +6, frequent association; 0, average; −1 to −6, less frequent; −7 to −12, rare association with people who hear.

INDEX